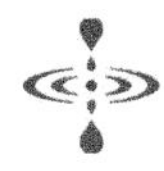

To take full advantage of this book, pl
the guided meditations, which ca

https://brightonmindfulnescentre.com/tpbook

First published in Great Britain in 2018 by Zen 23

zen23.co.uk

INTRODUCTION

Welcome to The Turning Point!

The first thing to say is thank you for choosing this book which is designed to work in tandem with our online mindfulness-based Turning Point course.

We believe that, if you use this course as intended, it has the potential to radically change your life.

By 'as intended', we mean that this book is essentially experiential. You need to actually DO the exercises and meditations, and follow the suggestions as closely as you can. Over time, after the course has finished, you'll doubtless tailor the exercises to fit your specific personal needs. But for now, we'd ask that you make a leap of faith that this stuff actually works and live the course rather than just reading about it or seeing it as some kind of cerebral box-ticking.

There is a wealth of scientific evidence that mindfulness can help you in all kinds of ways, both on our website at

brightonmindfulnesscentre.com and across the internet, with more emerging all the time. That's how a couple of old skeptics like us were convinced in the first place.

So take the plunge and be open to the possibilities.

If you read this book as some kind of theoretical exercise and then put it up on the bookshelf next to all the other books you've read in a similar fashion, then don't be too surprised if the benefits don't accrue. If you actively engage with the course and approach mindfulness with an open heart and a curious mind, then you'll be embarking on the adventure of a lifetime.

A Note On Transformation

Transformation tends to happen when we venture outside of our comfort zones. With The Turning Point, going beyond your comfort zone is always a gentle invitation, never a demand. It is left to you to decide whether to take up that invitation and be open to whatever arises. Almost certainly, it is when you gently stretch yourself in mindfulness practice that you will witness the most profound changes taking place.

Take mindful eating as an example. We are so hard-wired to wolf down our food as a secondary activity whilst we hold conversations, watch television, surf the net, plan our day, reflect on the day's events. We tend to barely notice the food we are consuming: how it looks, how it smells, its texture, even how it tastes. Mindful eating invites us to, even just once in a while, give the food we eat our full attention.

You'll probably find that, even if you get a lot out of a mindful eating exercise, you will wolf down your next meal as you've always done. This is OK. We are looking to build positives here, not damn negatives.

But we should also remember that the key to transformation is setting out with the intention of doing something differently, approaching it in a new way.

Slowly but surely, habits change. It probably won't be possible to eat every meal mindfully. Aiming for the impossible is not what mindfulness is about. Even if you manage to eat the occasional meal mindfully, there's every chance it will make a big difference to your life.

And it's worth remembering that, if you can eat a simple meal mindfully, even a bag of raisins, then you can do anything mindfully. Hopefully, that will becomes clearer and clearer as you proceed from week to week in the Turning Point course.

About This Mindfulness Course

Be assured that the course you have just begun has been carefully and deliberately assembled, using techniques developed over thousands of years, to equip you with new skills that can make a huge difference to your life.
The Turning Point is not a MBSR or MBCT course, although it contains elements of both.

Devised by Gerard Evans and Jon Wilde who jointly run the Brighton Mindfulness Centre, featuring key contributions from expert nutritionist Martina Watts, it is a unique mindfulness-based course geared towards firmly grounding you in the practice.

Gerard and Jon's lives have been radically transformed by mindfulness and they are firm believers that, with

application and patience, mindfulness can transform anybody's life.

We base our teaching on solid science and psychology and our aim is to make instruction as clear, practical and useful as possible.

On our courses you won't have to sit cross-legged (unless you really want to), you won't have to adopt the theologies of a religion (our approach is purely secular but not incompatible with any pre-existing beliefs) and you'll get instructions in plain English.

We don't expect you to practice for hours on end each day, nor to try and stop yourself from thinking (a sure recipe for struggle, failure and disappointment).

You'll be getting the strategies and information most suited to contemporary life. That is, techniques you can easily integrate into your day.

The great news is that the skills you learn on this course can easily be applied to just about any area of your life.

And, as you get to the end of the eighth week, if you wish to continue to be guided and supported in your practice, we have developed an ongoing Ninth Week course specifically for you. This is a course for the rest of your life. You'll find details of the Ninth Week course on our website brightonmindfulnesscentre.com.

Mindfulness, like any journey, begins with the first step. If you are ready to take that decisive, potentially life-changing step, if you are ready to walk the path of awakeness and awareness in your own way, our Turning Point course will gently guide you along, supporting you at every step.

We will show you how to live your life to the full, moment by moment.

As you will discover, learning to live mindfully involves a wealth of important lessons. Each lesson is, in its own way, a crucial turning point on your journey of self-discovery. Throughout the eight-week course, you'll find those turning points highlighted to make it easier for you to remember them.

This is not about looking to get some kind of experience you think is required as part of the course. This is about your experience as it is lived, moment to moment.
Perhaps the most crucial turning point of all is your decision to embark on the adventure in the first place. By choosing our course, you have already made that decision. So take a moment out to congratulate yourself for having reached that point.

INTRODUCTION TO MINDFULNESS

'When you change the way you look at things,
the things you look at change.'
- Wayne Dyer

In recent years the word 'mindfulness' has become almost as buzzed about as 'selfie' or 'tweet'. Some would go as far as to say that we are in the midst of a full-scale mindful revolution.

Certainly, more people than ever are opening themselves up to the practice of mindfulness-based meditation. It's been embraced by business leaders, politicians, pop stars and athletes; and recommended by doctors, clergy, psychotherapists and prison wardens.

Organisations that have enthusiastically adopted mindfulness include Google, Facebook, Twitter, Ford Motor Company, Goldman Sachs and the US Marines.

To coin a 60s phrase, mindfulness is currently 'all the rage' and shows no sign of losing momentum, on a global level.

For thousands of years, contemplative/meditative traditions have recommended mindful practice in a variety of forms to cultivate wellbeing in an individual's life. But, until fairly recently, meditation was generally viewed as something that belonged in the kooky margins, a throwback to the late 1960s when The Beatles hung out in Rishikesh with Maharishi Mahesh Yogi and sandal-wearing, right-on hippies turned inwards with the help of TM (transcendental meditation) and LSD.

Then, in the spring of 1979, a 35-year-old American molecular biologist, Jon Kabat-Zinn, was on a two-week meditation retreat when he had an epiphany that would have far-reaching aftereffects. While he sat alone one afternoon, it came to him that the people with chronic health problems

at his Massachusetts clinic might benefit greatly from meditation.

This was the moment that set Kabat-Zinn on the road to become the principal architect of mindfulness as we now know it. In time, Kabat-Zinn's mindfulness model would, for millions across the world, become the remedy of choice for the epidemic stress of modern life and countless other conditions.

Though Kabat-Zinn had received some Buddhist training in his twenties, he decided, in order to be all-inclusive, that the meditation-based practice would be taught in an entirely secular way. In other words, this modern form of mindfulness would be entirely free from religious/spiritual connotations.

Since then, Kabat-Zinn has repeatedly pointed out in books and interviews that there is nothing exclusively Eastern or Buddhist about mindfulness - paying attention in the moment is a universal human capacity.

Back in 1979, Kabat-Zinn founded the Stress Reduction & Relaxation Program at the University of Massachusetts

Medical School. The program would later be renamed Mindfulness-Based Stress Reduction (MBSR).

The 8-week MBSR course, introducing sitting meditations, body scans and mindful movement (a form of light yoga) became the standard way of delivering mindfulness to groups for many years until being joined by the 8-week Mindfulness-Based Cognitive Therapy (MBCT) course which marries traditional cognitive behavioral therapy methods to secular mindfulness approaches.

The MBCT course was developed specifically for recurrent depression but was found to substantially reduce the likelihood of repeated cycles of depressed mood.

As with MBSR, MBCT has also been proven to help with a wide array of other conditions, from common mental health problems (anxiety, eating disorders) to longstanding difficulties, severe mental illness, and physical problems including chronic pain and illness.

As Kabat-Zinn predicted, these course models have since been adopted by thousands of medical centres, hospitals and clinics around the world.

Nearly forty years on from the inception of Kabat-Zinn's clinic, mindfulness now sits comfortably with mainstream medicine, healthcare, cognitive science, neuroscience and education.

The evidence base is growing all the time and it is overwhelmingly persuasive in terms of its effectiveness in alleviating human suffering.

Mindfulness is now used for a massive range of medical conditions including cancer, heart disease, diabetes, brain injuries, fibromyalgia, HIV/Aids, Parkinson's, organ transplants, psoriasis, irritable bowel syndrome and tinnitus.

It is commonly used in the treatment of attention-deficit hyperactivity disorder, depression, chronic anxiety, panic attacks, obsessive-compulsive disorder, personality disorders, substance abuse and autism.

But mindfulness isn't only useful if you're feeling stressed, have a mental health problem or suffer from chronic pain. Its potential for catalysing profound learning, growing,

healing and personal transformation is vast and far-reaching.

It can help any of us enjoy a more wakeful, healthier, happier life, a life turned towards experience rather than away, a life of connection rather than alienation, a life travelled lightly rather than weighed down with fears and anxieties.

Mindfulness wakes us up to a true sense of intimacy with life.

Like many others, perhaps you have spent most of your life longing for that certain something that would bring you a greater contentment and peace of mind, that would make you more comfortable inside your own skin, that would help you cope more skillfully with challenging life situations.

That certain something has been inside you all along. It just needed to be noticed, and cultivated.

So what is mindfulness?

Teacher/writer Christina Feldman defines mindfulness as, 'the willingness and capacity to be equally present with all events and experiences with discernment, curiosity and kindness.'

Simply put, mindfulness is about awareness. The capacity to be with your experience, non-judgmentally, as it unfolds.

Mindfulness enables us to be present in our own lives. It offers a healthy alternative to living our lives 'inside our heads', forever at the mercy of our thoughts.

Turning point: When we are being mindful, we are paying attention in the present moment to things as they are rather than losing ourselves in thoughts about how we would prefer things to be.

By consciously directing our attention to our present moment experience, we become grounded. If we are aware

in the moment, we are able to choose how to respond adroitly to our situation rather than react unconsciously.

Thus, decisions are more likely to be made from a place of relative calm than from a state of deep worry or blind panic.

As we develop a more open, more intimate way of relating to body sensations, thoughts and feelings, we wake up to our experience rather than sleepwalking our way through our lives. We begin living without the weight of anxiety, depression, self-doubt, self-criticism, low self-esteem and social awkwardness.

We stop feeling overwhelmed by thoughts, feelings and body sensations. We can begin living with some peace of mind, comfortable in our own bodies, no longer feeling separate and isolated in the world. Whatever is happening in our lives at any moment, we can approach our situation with equanimity and serenity.

What mindfulness is not

It's not about stopping your thoughts - a very common misconception.

Nor is it about achieving a certain state. For example, relaxation is often a very pleasant by-product of mindfulness practice but mindfulness is not a relaxation therapy. Not exactly.

Feeling more relaxed is one of the many welcome by-products of mindfulness practice. But we don't meditate in order to feel relaxed.

Confused? Look at it this way...

If you do a relaxation exercise and you feel other than relaxed at the end of it, you would probably feel a sense of disappointment, even failure. But, if we are being mindful, what matters is that we are paying attention to our experience and being with it as it unfolds. Simply noticing whatever comes up – be it pleasant, unpleasant, or something in between - rather than turning away from it, wishing it would recede from our experience.

At all times, what we think and do is determined to a large degree by what we fail to notice. If we are noticing, paying attention, we cannot fail at mindfulness. If we are turning up in our own lives, we cannot be doing mindfulness wrong.

Imagine the following scenario.

You are on holiday, walking along a sea front on a beautifully sunny summer's day. There is so much that you could be bringing your attention to: the sandy beach; the noise of children playing; the gentle forward movement of the waves; the reggae music joyfully booming from a pair of speakers; the heady scent of cold vinegar cascading onto hot chips wrapped in newspaper.

However, you are completely immersed in thoughts about what your father-in-law said to you at the fete last week… and in thoughts about how you never enjoy meeting the in-laws as you feel judged by them…and you start wondering what your in-laws really think about you…and then you begin wondering what your friends really think of you…and the memory arises of that kid at school who called you an

idiot even though you'd never knowingly done anything to deserve the insult…then there was the time…

Meanwhile, you are barely aware of anything the beautiful summer's day has to offer. Your experience has narrowed itself down to a stream of gloom-ridden thoughts.

Now imagine this scenario.

You are in a restaurant, having lunch with a friend you have not seen for some time. You are delighted to see them but, halfway through the meal, your thoughts drift towards the meeting with your boss the following day. There have been a few redundancies at the firm recently. Maybe you are next in line for the chop? If you lose your job, how will you pay your mortgage? If your house is repossessed, what will become of you? Will you end up living on the streets, picking through waste bins for something to eat…? What will become of your wife and two kids? Will all your friends desert you?

Lost in the chain-reaction of thoughts, you barely notice the taste of the food you are eating and the wine you are drinking. You are barely aware of what your friend is saying

to you. When you return home later and your partner asks you how the lunch went, you have scant recollection of anything that happened or anything that was said. You can barely remember any of the worries and concerns that swept your attention away like leaves on a stormy day.

You get the picture. When your attention is snatched away by thoughts about the past or the future, you are not participating in the present moment. You are somewhere else. In a sense, your body is in one place, your mind in another. The gap between your body and mind then becomes a fertile breeding ground for feelings of anxiety and general unease.

The fact is that, no matter how hard we try, we cannot influence the past. Nor can we influence the future.

We can learn from the past but we cannot reside there. Furthermore, we don't need to dwell on past events as though they are happening in the here and now. With this realisation, we can give up on efforts to rewrite the past.

We can plan wisely for the future but thoughts about the future should not paralyse us with worry and fear. We might

think we know how the future is going to unfold, but the truth is that we can never be certain. At best, the future is an educated guess.

Mindfulness teaches us to be with our experience in the present moment. It also teaches us not to expect the present moment to be a certain way. When you accept your experience fully, you are much less likely,to get caught up in it, be defined by it, or feel overwhelmed by it.

Most of us will be familiar with the feeling of being 'miles away', lost in thought and unaware of our surroundings. According to experts, our minds wander at least 50% of the time, which sounds like a conservative estimate. Either way, for at least 50% of the time, we are on auto-pilot, acting without conscious intention. In other words, we are not aware of what we are doing while we are doing it.

It's perfectly normal for your mind to wander. Mindfully speaking, the important thing is realising it, then bringing your attention back to what is occurring in the present moment.

Research has shown that people are less happy when their minds are wandering than when they are focussing on what they are doing. Thinking about what is not happening makes us more unhappy than paying attention to what is happening.

Doing some things automatically, without having to think too hard about them, can sometimes be an advantage. Driving a car would be exhausting if, every time you got behind the wheel, you had to think carefully about where the clutch pedal, throttle and brake pedal were located.

But, if you live your life on automatic, you miss what is going on around you.

If our wandering thoughts amounted only to occasional bouts of harmless daydreaming, there wouldn't be a problem. But our minds seem to be primed to focus on negative rather than positive stimuli and it is all too easy to get drawn into negative spirals of thinking.

It's as though we are programmed as human beings to seek pleasure but it is the unpleasant stuff that detains us. We

seem to have a natural tendency to hold on to unpleasant experiences, to dwell on the negative.

The brain's bias has been described as 'Velcro for negative experiences and Teflon for positive experiences.'

Happy thoughts come and go. But bleak ruminations about the past or speculative thoughts about life as a series of potential dangers can lock us into a state of never-ending anxiety that can be highly detrimental to our health.

I've suffered a great many catastrophes in my life. Most of them never happened."
- Mark Twain

Mindfulness can go a long way toward helping us change these thinking habits. Being mindfully aware rather than being on automatic pilot allows for the possibility of freedom from the mechanical, reactive, habitual patterns of mind.

Scientific research has consistently shown that regular mindfulness practice can reshape the mind so that it is naturally geared towards greater emotional equilibrium and therefore greater happiness and wellbeing.

Until a few decades ago, scientists were convinced that our brains were fundamentally unchangeable.

Subsequent research has established that neurons and neural networks in the brain change their connections and behaviour in response to new information, environment and experience.

The brain changes both structure and function depending on how we pay attention and what we pay attention to.

Numerous studies have shown that participating in an 8-week mindfulness course such as this one brings about measurable changes in brain regions associated with memory, emotion regulation and stress, and brings lasting cognitive and psychological benefits.

So much of our lives seems to be spent trying to get, or wishing we were, somewhere else. Anywhere but where we actually are in the present moment.

★

Turning point: Ultimately, mindfulness isn't really about getting anywhere. It's about being where we are right now, opening to our experience just as it is.

So many of us spend a great deal of our lives wishing that the present moment was other than it is. We want the moment to be brighter or shinier. We don't want to be feeling the way we are. We don't want the moment we are experiencing. We want the moment he is having, or the one she is having. And so on.

The stark fact is that the present moment has already arrived. If we try to wish it away, we are engaged in a futile fight with the universe.

It's as though we believe that we can step outside of life's natural flow and manipulate the universe so that we get exactly what we want every time.

The universe is not ours to control. And wanting things to be pleasurable all the time, wanting to be happy all the time,

are impossible fantasies that only lead to frustration and discontent.

Besides, the word 'happy' comes from the same root as 'to happen'. So you could say that to experience happiness means to participate whole-heartedly in whatever is happening right now and to feel whatever is arising. Which is as good a definition of mindfulness as any.

Think about all your great experiences in life and you'll notice they were all times when you were fully in the present moment. You won't be thinking about great times you had when you were looking forward to things.

We tend to buy into the idea that certain things in life will bring us lasting happiness: the ideal partner, money in the bank, the perfect job. When we are not happy, we tend to look outside of ourselves for things to blame for the fact that we are not content. Our partner doesn't measure up. We don't have enough money. Our job is unfulfilling.

We convince ourselves that happiness, lasting happiness, will come just as soon as we get the things we want. Then,

as soon as we get those things, we find that the cycle repeats itself.

It doesn’t seem to occur to us that our lack of contentment may have something to do with the fact that we are living for some future moment, rather than finding meaning and contentment in the simplicity of living, breathing and being.

We seem to spend so much of our lives stiffly braced against life’s inevitabilities, as if worrying about things will ward off the unwelcome and the unpleasant. But there is a more skilful way to live, one given to responding more skilfully when difficulties arise.

This principle is illustrated by an ancient parable about the pine and the willow in heavy snow. The pine branch, being rigid, cracks under the weight of the snow; but the springy willow branch yields to the weight, and the snow drops off. Mindfulness teaches us to live life more like the willow than the pine, and to notice the difference.

Mindfulness will not completely eliminate life's pressures and it will not solve all our problems, but it can help us

respond to them in a calmer, more resourceful, more conscious manner.

Mindfulness doesn't pretend that it will take you to a place where everything is just as you would like it. That place does not exist and has never existed.

Instead, it offers an alternative to turning away from the experiences we instantly label as unpleasant or unwelcome.

The idea of turning directly towards difficult thoughts and emotional pain would sound counter-intuitive to most people. But haven't we all found that turning away from these thoughts or emotions hasn't solved anything? It hasn't even protected us.

When we learn to turn towards experience, opening ourselves to challenging experiences, strong impulses and physical cravings, we allow ourselves not to be swept away by habitual patterns. We learn to recognize those habits when they arise and, with that kind recognition, they tend to loosen their hold on us.

Instead of being swept away, we return our attention to the present moment which is, of course, the only moment we actually have. It is sometimes easy to forget that the time is always now. Mindfulness teaches us that we have a choice: whether to be aware of what is unfolding in our minds, bodies and the world around us; or to be somewhere else.

We can think about the past and think about the future but only from the standpoint of the present moment.
Mindfulness allows us to be right there, inhabiting the moment fully, letting ourselves be.

For many of us, everyday life can often narrow itself down to little more than a list of pressing demands, things to tick off as we go about our day. If we can take a mindful pause once in a while, we might ask ourselves, 'Where am I on this list? What am I giving to myself?'

And it's not just about you. When we begin to lay the foundations for mindful living, we become more tuned in to the wellbeing of others. Traditionally, in meditation circles, compassion is viewed as the noblest quality of the human heart, the motivation underlying all paths of healing and personal transformation.

Mindfulness is as much about becoming more compassionate to others as it is about self-compassion. What we practice, we cultivate. If we practice being kind and caring, we will become kinder and more caring.

With practice we learn to meet our own suffering and that of others with kindness, patience, equanimity and, crucially, without judgment.

With compassion, we can approach our own suffering and that of others with a more generous, more open heart. When we are compassionate, when we experience loving-kindness, we see that every one of us shares the same wish to be healthy and happy, to be in touch with our intrinsic wholeness, to transcend fear and despair. We learn to appreciate our common humanity.

We start to notice that all unpleasant behaviour, in ourselves and others, is born of pain and fear. With this on board, we can learn to react more considerately and less judgmentally to that which we find unpleasant. This in turn, rewards us with a greater inner peace.

When we start practising mindfulness, we're embarking on a journey that helps us connect, to live life more fully, and to realize our full potential as conscious and compassionate beings.

With practice, we learn to fold mindfulness into our daily lives so that being mindful becomes second nature. We learn to be instinctively more awake in our daily lives. Practice is a commitment to openness, a saying no to avoidance.

It takes courage to say, 'I refuse to live this way any longer.' But it doesn't have to be difficult. You just need to be ready, to be open, to be receptive to whatever arises moment to moment, accepting that this is what life is presenting to you right now.

You might find yourself asking, 'Do I have time for this?' It might be more worthwhile to ask, 'Do I have the time to show up in my own life?'

If you tell yourself that you don't have time to meditate at least for a few minutes each day, then maybe it's time to start looking at what makes your life so frantically busy.

Maybe it is time to start making time for being fully present in your life, rather than simply cramming activities into your day.

Do bear in mind that mindfulness doesn't promise a quick fix. It requires patience, self-compassion, a certain amount of commitment, a certain amount of motivation, and a willingness to be open to change. Consistency of practice also helps. Some people take to it quickly. Others less so. Everyone's mindfulness journey is unique.

Over the forthcoming weeks, it is likely that you will experience moments of frustration, irritation, boredom, self-doubt and even stern resistance. That's OK. Recognising and accepting those experiences is an important and helpful part of the practice.

Bear in mind that mindfulness is much more than a set of useful techniques. Mindfulness cultivates a whole new way of being. We practice, and we practice some more. If our practice lapses, we form the intention to try again.
Slowly, but unmistakably, mindfulness becomes a way of being. Less and less do we need to deliberately be mindful in a situation. Mindfulness becomes our default position.

Mindfulness is a great adventure. Make it the centre line in your life, and reap the benefits.

Enjoy it and do make the most of it.

Hopefully it will be as life-changing for you as it has been for us.

INTRODUCTION TO NUTRITION

As a society, we are preoccupied, even to the point of obsession, with eating properly, yet so many of us are inadequately nourished and so many of us appear to have a problematic relationship with food.

Most of us are under no illusions about the connection between poor diet and poor health though we might choose to turn a blind eye to some of the more discomforting links between diet and disease. The stark truth is that four of the top ten causes of death today (coronary heart disease, diabetes, stroke and cancer) have long-established links to diet.

The worldwide prevalence of obesity more than doubled between 1980 and 2014. Research has shown that more than two billion people worldwide are now overweight or obese. The US has 13% of the world's overweight population, a greater percentage than any other country.

In the past three decades, no country has been able to curb obesity rates.

There are plenty of 'experts' out there ready and willing to explain where we are all going wrong but the advice they give is often contradictory and nearly always confusing.

We are bombarded by the blatant propaganda of the food-marketing industry. We are swayed one way and then another by newspaper reports about nutrition that seem to have more to do with making cheap headlines than telling us the truth.

We are left bewildered by the constantly shifting advice of nutrition science. What is promoted as healthy in one decade is dismissed as potentially deadly in the next.

No sooner are we over the excitement of being told that a low-fat diet protects against cancer than we learn that it does no such thing. First we learn that dietary fibre helps prevent heart disease. Then we find…well, you get the picture. No wonder most of us are in a state of extreme nutritional stupefaction.

As Michael Pollan writes in his iconoclastic book, In Defence Of Food, 'All of our uncertainties about nutrition should not obscure the plain fact that the chronic diseases that now kill most of us can be traced directly to the industrialisation of our food: the rise of highly processed foods and refined grains; the use of chemicals to raise plants and animals in huge monocultures; the superabundance of cheap calories of sugar and fat produced by modern agriculture; and the narrowing of the biological diversity of the human diet to a tiny handful of staple crops – notably wheat, corn and soy.

These changes have given us the Western diet that we take for granted: lots of processed foods and meat, lots of added fat and sugar, lots of everything – except vegetables, fruit and whole grains.'

Given all that, the solution would appear to be easy. We need to be more careful about what we put in our mouths every day. No junk food. Fewer animal products and fewer processed foods. Less refined carbohydrates. More plants, vegetables and legumes. More fresh fruit. More whole grains. More water. Less alcohol, less sugary drinks and 'energy' drinks.

But, of course, it's not that easy. Not least because all of us are different. Your body reflects a complex, interrelated system that includes your unique mix of genetics, allergies, hormones, desires, appetite, mood, emotions, physical makeup, and much more. Finding out what foods or dietary system is best for you takes time and patience.

Another factor is that, for most of us, dietary habits are deeply ingrained, and have been for a long while, perhaps since early childhood. Along the way, perhaps we have forgotten that, in addition to providing our body with its daily fuel, eating can be and should be one of the greatest joys in life.

Instead, maybe eating is now something that we squeeze into our day. It's something we do between stopping one activity and starting another. How many of our meals are consumed 'on the run'? How often do we eat whilst gazing at television or gawping at a smartphone screen? How many of us eat lunch at our desks rather than take a proper break? How often do we eat simply because it's time to eat rather than because we are answering the call of hunger? How often do we bolt our food down without tasting it properly? How often do we eat completely on auto-pilot, barely even aware that we are eating?

Perhaps eating has become a routine, even unconscious activity for many of us.

If we are intent upon eating more nutritiously, we don't necessarily need to take giant steps. Perhaps a series of small steps might be more easily manageable.

Maybe we could start by simply rediscovering the joy of eating by being more present at each stage of a meal, from deciding what it is that we want to eat to washing up and tidying away.

If we can start eating mindfully and self-compassionately, become conscious of what we are consuming, perhaps we will discover not only that mindful eating is an integral part of healthy eating but also that mindful eating leads to mindful living.

SESSION ONE: JUST NOTICING

'Just to welcome our life as it arrives moment after moment, to meet it as fully as we can, being as open to it as we can, being as ready for whatever arises as we can, and meeting it wholeheartedly, this is renunciation - this is leaving behind all of our preferences, all of our ideas and notions and schemes. Just meeting life as it is.'
Blanche Hartman: Seeds For A Boundless Life

'Be with what is, as it is.'
Jon Bernie

Theme For Session One

On this course we will be exploring two areas in particular.

The first is paying attention. The second is cultivating compassion for ourselves and others.

Roughly speaking, the first half of this Turning Point course will be spent honing the muscles of awareness, exploring how we pay attention, where we put our attention, and how that affects our moment to moment experience. The second half of the course will be more concerned with compassion and turning, with compassion, towards difficulties.

In this first session, you will be introduced to three different meditations that, in their various ways, are concerned with 'just noticing'.

With the raisin exercise, the sitting/breathing meditation and the sitting/breathing/body meditation, we are learning different ways to anchor our awareness in the moment - using as our focus of attention the raisin, the breath and key parts of the body.

When we notice what is happening in the moment, it is very possible that we are able to respond wisely rather than react impulsively to whatever life presents. We give ourselves the possibility of greater freedom and choice. Hopefully we can avoid getting trapped on the same old assembly line of well-worn habits.

It is likely that we have lived with these habits for so long they have become ingrained, so much so that we are unaware that they are being acted out again and again and again.

Of course, not all habits are bad habits. But habits rooted in self-criticism, blame, selfishness and anger, will cause suffering for ourselves and others if they go unchecked.

Turning point: In simply noticing when a habit is triggered, we are far less likely to identify with it or act it out. Every time you make a mindful choice or go against long-established habits, the easier it will be to do the same thing subsequently.

In time, the layers of habit peel off. Perhaps then, a new habit can be cultivated: the habit of being present in your own life.

Mindfulness teaches us that what we notice from moment to moment makes a profound difference to our sense of wellbeing. As the saying goes: Where attention goes, energy flows.

You can work on undoing an unhealthy habit by focusing your attention at three distinct times:

Before: Forming the intention of paying attention the next time you find yourself engaging in the habit. Reminding yourself that, when the urge arises to indulge a habit, you have a choice as to whether you enact the habitual behaviour or whether you act mindfully. This intention doesn't have to weigh heavily on you. Carry it lightly, like a butterfly alighting on your shoulder.

During: When that urge arises, you can allow yourself to be open to the experience of feelings, sensations and thoughts, then choose not to indulge the habitual behaviour.

After: If you went ahead and engaged the habit, accept that fact with self-compassion. Acknowledge that you at least made a commitment to be mindful. Remind yourself that, if

you keep your intention oriented, you can bring attention to the habit the next time it arises.

Think about this. How often do we pay attention, close attention, in our everyday lives? We might walk through a beautiful park and register that the scenery is lovely, but how much attention are we actually paying?

When sitting on a plane, we might occasionally divert our attention from the movie we're watching and glance through the windows at the cloud formations.

We might even think, 'Hmm, nice clouds.' But how much attention are we bringing to the moment. Are we really noticing? Is it possible to bring our full attention to these wonders of nature? Can we take the time to look, really look?

'We shall not cease from exploration
And the end of all our exploring
Will be to arrive where we started
And know the place for the first time.' (T.S. Eliot)

Noticing matters. Every moment is surely deserving of our attention and consideration. What unexpected wonders will be waiting if you really look and listen? How will moments of beauty and moments of joy find you if you are not paying attention? If your mind is elsewhere?

If you change your attention, you change your experience. With practice, we can bring a fresh quality of attention to any experience, in any situation, at any time of the day. Just by paying attention, we can shift from where we think we are, to where we really are, and we can then attend to our lives in this moment.

Consider the story told in his memoir (An Evil Cradling) by Brian Keenan, the Irish teacher held hostage for many months in Lebanon during the 1980s. Keenan recalls how an orange found its way onto his meal tray one day. In the darkness and dire loneliness of his solitary confinement, the sight of the orange brought Keenan to his knees in tears and wonder. He couldn't bear to eat it for a long time. For days he simply regarded it with gratitude. It was as if he was looking at an orange for the very first time.

As Keenan writes, ‘My eyes are almost burned by what I see. The fruit, the colours, mesmerize me in a quiet rapture that spins through my head…I lift an orange into the flat, filthy palm of my hand and feel and smell and lick it. The colour orange, the colour, the colour, my God the colour orange. Before me is a feast of colour. I feel myself begin to dance, slowly, I am intoxicated by colour... Such wonder, such absolute wonder in such insignificant fruit. I cannot, I will not eat this fruit. I sit in quiet joy, so completely beyond the meaning of joy. My soul finds its own completeness in that bowl of colour…I want to bow before it, loving that blazing, roaring, orange colour…In there, in that tiny bowl, the world recreated in that tiny bowl…I focus all of my attention on that bowl of fruit…I cannot hold the ecstacy of the moment and its passionate intensity…I am filled with a sense of love.’

This story is worth remembering the next time we find ourselves wolfing down food without paying any attention to how it looks, smells and tastes. We don’t need to be brought to our knees in tearful wonder every time a plate of food is put in front of us.

But maybe we can eat a little more consciously. By waking up and noticing, maybe we can live more consciously. By living more consciously, more mindfully, so the quality of our life improves proportionately.

Show up. Slow down. Settle in.
It's not much more complicated than that.

Home practice for week following session one

Sitting/Breathing Meditation

Listen to the Sitting/Breathing Meditation on three days out of the next seven. Give yourself one day off. Notice the difference when you go a day without practicing. Use the workbook pages at the end of this chapter to record your experience each time you listen to the track.

Sitting/Breathing/Body Meditation

Listen to the Sitting/Breathing/Body Meditation on three days out of the next seven. Give yourself one day off. Notice the difference when you go a day without practicing.

Use the workbook pages at the end of this chapter to record your experience each time you listen to the track.

Mindful Activity

Choose one routine activity in your daily life and make a deliberate effort to bring moment-to-moment awareness to that activity each time you do it, just as we did in the raisin exercise. Possibilities include brushing your teeth, taking a shower, getting dressed, driving to work, shopping etc. Simply bring your attention to what you are doing as you are doing it, and notice when your attention is pulled elsewhere.

NUTRITION - Week One

Nutrition As An Integral Component Of Mindfulness Practice

Most of us would agree, when pressed, that nutrition is the foundation for good health and provides us with the resources we need to build strong and resilient bodies. The human brain, just like any other organ in the body, also requires adequate nourishment to function and perform as it should.

Our brains not only regulate many key processes in our bodies, but also act as the home-base of our minds. Under the day-to-day pressures of modern life, we tend to forget this and just fuel our brains with whatever lies conveniently to hand, without regard to the physical, mental and spiritual consequences. We may be feeding our bodies, but not nourishing our minds.

The incidence of mood and stress-related disorders is growing at an alarming rate, and the number of prescriptions for antidepressants is soaring, including those for children. Many of us are content with the 'pill for an ill' paradigm, ignoring the link between our own consumptive habits and the way we feel.

We do know from experience and usually to our cost, that alcohol or drug addiction affects our mood, behaviour and judgment. But to what extent does our daily diet influence how we think and behave?

In a perfect world, if the optimal nutritional requirements for the human brain could be established, would we be able to tone down our stressful thoughts, improve mood and cognitive performance, reduce aggressive or violent behaviour - or even treat mental health problems? The consensus amongst nutritional professionals is that we must honour the dietary requirements of the brain and if we don't, the broad consequences are entirely predictable.

The official advice, however, to "just eat a healthy balanced diet" is at least half a century out of date. What exactly is it that we are supposed to balance? Should we mix'n'match different pesticide residues in our food or change our preferred brand of flavoured crisps?

The processed convenience food we now eat contains artificial additives and chemicals, and even the most sophisticated computer can't calculate whether consumers are affected by their long-term cumulative effects.

All we can say, with absolute certainty, is that our bodies did not evolve to gain nourishment or benefit from man-made food-substitutes - and that the most likely outcome of such consumption (aside from inflating the bank balances of 'Big-Food' companies) is a mind and body under constant stress and confusion.

Our diet is no longer 'compatible' with that of our ancestors. Hunter-gatherers depended on seasonal consumption of whole, fresh and unrefined 'brain food': plenty of different fruit and vegetables, nuts, seeds, legumes and some oily fish and lean meat.

Now, our bodies have to cope with a high glycaemic load year-round from sugars and refined grain products, high salt, a lack of omega-3 fats, an overload of processed and damaged fats and many other factors. These modern dietary characteristics do not provide us with the ingredients for long-term health for either mind or body.

Even if we shop at the fresh vegetable section, we are not risk-free. Our produce has suffered heavy mineral losses. Over a 51-year period between 1940 and 1991, vegetables, on average, have lost about half their calcium content and a quarter of their iron and magnesium content, with even greater losses for zinc. It is well accepted that mineral deficiencies can have a profound impact on our mental and emotional health.

"You are what you eat"... I'm sure you have heard the saying. Any Nutritional Therapist worth their salt will tell you this is not strictly true. We should be under no illusion that a healthy diet alone will cure us of all ills, because you aren't just what you eat, but what your body is able to digest and do with the food that you do eat.

Complex processes are involved in the selection of food, and a well-functioning digestive tract and healthy gut flora are required to break down and absorb nutrients, and efficiently dispose of pathogens or toxic substances.

The immune system is important, too: inflammatory responses to a psychological factor like stress, or a physical threat in form of a virus or bacteria, can lead to prolonged bouts of depression or anxiety.

Today's health problems are largely based on underlying biochemical imbalances caused by our diet and the environment we live in. A toxic lifestyle, allergies, addictions, stress and bugs can be far more damaging to our health than the genes we inherited – and as the reasons behind the current crisis in mental and emotional health are so diverse, we need an integrated approach to managing them.

I grew up in an age when it was common to speak a short prayer before eating, and speaking during meals was kept to a minimum. Eating was not always just a speedy and functional necessity – it occupied a separate and unique space in one's daily routine, a peaceful anchor point to the world around us. In today's more secular context, this is mindful eating.

This online course includes nutritional strategies that will support your mindfulness practice as well as your long-term health.

The mindful eating of a raisin is a wonderful first exercise in becoming aware of the myriad of mechanical and chemical processes involved in the digestive process, where food is broken up into smaller and simpler parts that can be absorbed and assimilated. Each new weekly session will equip you with practical suggestions you can use at once – all without overwhelming you or breaking the bank. Enjoy!

Jon's Reflections On Week One

Reflections on the raisin exercise

I remember being at my first ever mindfulness session and being asked to close my eyes and open the palm of one hand. When I reopened my eyes, there sat a solitary raisin.

My first thought was 'This is a little odd', followed by, 'Maybe this mindfulness thing is not for me.'

The penny dropped a little while into the exercise. I could see that this was simply about paying attention.

In the inquiry following the exercise, I recall saying to the teacher that, whenever I'd eaten dried fruit before, I'd tended to shovel it down my throat as quickly as possible.

That I could easily get through a whole bag of raisins without noticing anything about the experience of eating them - the taste, the smell, the texture…and that I did that with a lot of food.

But eating that raisin was different. I was aware at every stage. At least most of the time. My attention wandered a little. Mostly, I was focussed. And, when I finally got to taste the raisin, it was delicious. Tastier than any raisin I've ever tried, even though I was aware that I was eating a perfectly normal raisin, the kind you can find in any budget supermarket.

The whole experience made me very curious. If I could be mindful about something as simple as eating a single raison, what else could I be mindful about? Maybe everything?

That was the moment that I realized I would give mindfulness my best shot.

Since that first session, I've not always found it easy to eat mindfully. Old habits don't always give themselves up easily. Occasionally I still find myself reading a newspaper or gazing at a television screen at mealtimes.

And that's OK. I don't give myself a hard time about it. Quite often, I find my mind wandering off when I'm eating. That's OK too. I simply register the fact that my mind has

wandered and bring my attention back to the taste of the food.

I’ve learned that it helps to form the intention to be mindful before sitting down to a meal. Or, if I’m cooking it myself, to form the intention to be mindful as I chop the ingredients etc.

Perhaps the most crucial thing I’ve learned is that, yes, if one can be mindful about eating a raisin, one can be mindful about anything. Absolutely anything.

Reflections on the sitting/breathing meditation

Quite honestly, I found this a little challenging at first. When my teacher first mentioned my mind wandering during the meditation, I realised that it was all over the place, regularly flitting off into thoughts about the past and the future. I was quite taken aback at how busy my mind was. It felt like a pinball machine at full pelt.

I was greatly encouraged when my teacher remarked that the fact my mind was wandering didn't mean I was doing it wrong.

As the meditation went on, it felt a bit easier to just concentrate on the breath. I remember feeling a genuine sense of achievement when I noticed, without prompting, that my mind had wandered and I came back to the breath.

Over subsequent weeks, I kept up the daily practice and noticed that it became easier and easier to keep my attention trained on the breath. Sure, there were days when my mind was busier than others, but I learned to accept that as normal.

I found that the more I practiced, the more thoughts seemed to lose their momentum, lose their hold on me.

Reflections on the sitting/breathing/body meditation

One of the preconceptions I brought to mindfulness was that it was all about stilling the mind by stopping thoughts. I've since learned this is a fairly common misconception. The sitting/breathing/body meditation also alerted me to the fact

that mindfulness is as much about body awareness as awareness of mental activity.

Bringing my attention to my feet, my lower legs etc. was something entirely new to me. The truth is that I had very rarely been aware of body sensations, apart from everyday pains, strains and itches. Even then, I hadn't brought my curiosity to bear on what was being felt. I just wanted to get rid of the sensations as quickly as possible and feel 'normal' again.

This meditation offered a glimpse of what it was like to simply be with sensations, to hold them in awareness for a few moments, to accept that they had already arrived – whether I liked them or not.

Admittedly, I wasn't able to notice sensations in all areas of my body. There was a little tingling in my feet and a little soreness in the small of my back, but nothing seemed to be going on in my knees or my arms. I found this frustrating. But I was reassured by my teacher saying that, if no sensations were felt, to simply register 'no sensations'.

As time goes on, I’ve found it easier and easier to tune into my body, noticing even the most subtle sensations, and allowing them to be.

Gerard's Reflections On Week One

Meditation

I feel like, even in a 5 minute meditation, I'm actually doing nothing for the first time in my adult life! My usual version of “doing nothing” or “having a break” simply involves going on Facebook or watching TV or just planning the future or worrying about the past. It’s only when I actually do nothing that I realise I wasn’t giving my brain a break at all, I wasn’t even slowing down! No wonder I was always tired.

Finally I’m being nice to myself and finding that I’m able to take a genuine rest. The raisin exercise felt bizarre and difficult at the start, so conditioned am I to gulping down food. But, towards the end, it was as if the whole universe and time itself had slowed down to a pace I was far more comfortable with.

One of the biggest challenges for me with the meditations was getting over the idea I was wasting valuable time - time I could be spending doing something USEFUL. Being self-employed as I am, it’s easy to fall into the trap of feeling

guilty every moment you're not trying to make money - particularly when you're on the breadline.

As time went on, and I meditated more, my perception changed in a couple of ways. The benefits of meditation made me realise I was able to focus on my work a lot better and my mind was generally a lot clearer.

So giving myself 20-30 minutes before work began in the morning to attain this clarity stopped feeling like wasted time and started feeling like an important investment.
Also, I realised I was looking forward to meditating like I looked forward to going to the pub - the intention might not be to feel better afterwards but it sure as hell was the result - even on days when the meditation was hard going, when thoughts wouldn't stop pummelling their way in. Those days, I reasoned, were the days I needed it most of all.

Nutrition

Almost immediately I found myself becoming more aware of what I was putting in my shopping basket and, indeed, what I was putting in my mouth. Unlike previous occasions, however, this wasn't a diet. This was, consciously, the rest

of my life. So I decided not giving myself a hard time about anything, Initially, I decided that just noticing was sufficient, like the raisin exercise.

And it was pretty amazing what I noticed. I was buying and eating so much on auto-pilot and consuming SO much processed food. For now, I maintained the idea: I'm not stopping, just noticing. But it felt inevitable that all this noticing would have a long-term effect on the contents of my kitchen cupboard and, therefore, my health and wellbeing.

FREQUENTLY ASKED QUESTIONS (FAQ) FOR WEEK ONE

My main problem in this first week of the course has been that I've felt a great deal of discomfort during the body scan. I seem to be aware of sensations I don't like all over my body. It's a real trial.

Do you have any tips for dealing with this?

Try staying with the discomfort a little longer than you normally would. Explore it with interest and curiosity. What is the exact nature of this discomfort? Is it constant? Or is it constantly changing?

Don't keep your attention trained on discomfort indefinitely, especially if it's becoming unbearable. If your experience is that extreme, maybe direct your attention to the breath, or make a slight adjustment to your posture so that you feel more comfortable.

I am new to mindfulness, five days into week one of this course. My question is about meditating on the breath.

When I'm conscious of my breathing, I am peaceful for three or four breaths, but I find it impossible to maintain that state of peace.
Am I doing it wrong?

Mindfulness is not about attaining/maintaining a specific state like relaxation. It's about being with whatever is arising in your experience in the present moment - pleasant, unpleasant or indifferent.

If certain breaths don't feel 'peaceful', that's fine, just be with what is. Notice when you are striving for a specific goal and let go of that.

Place your attention on what is being experienced in the moment, not on what you would like to feel in the moment. And do remind yourself that you are at an early stage of the practice. If you stick with it, you will start finding it easier to keep your attention focussed on the breath, without even trying.

I came to this course (recommended by a friend) after I'd done a four-week mindfulness course last summer. For a while after the course I managed to stick with the

practice and felt much calmer, much less anxious.

Now I'm struggling as, during meditations, I seem to be striving to achieve the kind of calm I felt during meditations last year.

I realise that I should be in the moment (not in last year's moment) but I'm finding it really difficult not to strive to replicate what I felt last year.
Any advice would be very much appreciated.

You are being mindful in the sense that you notice when you are striving to replicate the state that you experienced previously.

Try approaching every meditation as though it is your first. We call this 'beginner's mind'. Today's meditation is never going to be the same experience as yesterday's. Or, as they say in Zen, you can't step into the same river twice.
When you notice frustration or wishful thinking arising, simply notice that, then gently return your attention to the anchor of the breath.

I work quite long hours in my job and, already, a few days into the course, I'm finding it hard to stay awake during meditation - especially during the body scan which I lie down for.
Any ideas?

Especially during the early stages of the course, it's not uncommon for people to feel sleepy during the body scan.
Try simply noticing that you are feeling tired and adjust your posture if you think that will help.

Remind yourself that the aim is to fall awake, rather than fall asleep.

If tiredness during meditation continues, perhaps cultivate the intention of going to bed earlier and getting up earlier, then meditating before or straight after breakfast.
Also, perhaps ask yourself if you simply need more sleep generally.

I have been doing body scans for a few days now. On some parts of the body I don't feel any sensation. What's up?

Nothing is up. Don't worry. If you feel nothing at all, that is fine. Just register 'no sensation'.

Remember. In a body scan, we are not trying to change anything that's already there. If that big toe is itchy, we notice that it's itchy without getting caught up in thoughts of wishing it wasn't itchy. And so we learn to be with our experience without being drawn into thoughts about how our present moment experience ought to be.

I'm a confirmed atheist and I have been as far back as I can recall.

So here's the thing. I'm enjoying what I've seen of this course so far but it is slightly bothering me that I might be doing some kind of religious meditation. And Buddhism is a religion, right?

Assuredly, this course is entirely secular in nature and there ought to be no barriers to participation.

There is nothing exclusively Eastern or Buddhist about mindfulness - paying attention in the moment is a universal human capacity. Chances are it started with hunters way

back in our history, and as such, its roots would be universal, not Eastern.

As for Buddhism being a religion, opinion is divided on that. Many people believe that it is a philosophy rather than a religion. Either way, Buddhism has no bearing on what you are learning on this course.

I am a little confused by references I've come across to the different kind of mindfulness courses on the market. I've heard about MBCT and MBSR. What's the difference between them?

Also, what kind of mindfulness course is this that you are running? MBCT? MBSR? Or something else entirely?

MBCT (Mindfulness Based Cognitive Therapy) tends to target a specific condition whereas MBSR (Mindfulness Based Stress Reduction) is more generic and is applied to stress arising from a variety of life events.

MBCT puts a greater emphasis on working with and understanding the psychological and cognitive aspects of our experience.

Our course, The Turning Point, includes elements of MBCT and MBSR, in terms of structure if not content, but is essentially a stand-alone course.

I joined your course yesterday. How long will it take before I notice a difference in my life?

There are no quick fixes with mindfulness. Also, there is a good deal of variability in how this practice impacts and when people start to see any changes occur. Often, co-workers, family and friends sometimes notice these changes before we ourselves are clearly aware of them.
For now, just enjoy the practice for its own sake and try to put aside any thoughts about how quickly this is going to make a difference in your life.

I'm in my first week and facing some dilemmas. The biggest one is the inconsistency of my meditations.

?

Yesterday my meditation was easy and today it was hard. My mind just kept drifting away to my weekend plans and work issues. What am I doing wrong?

Assuredly, you are not doing anything wrong.

Some days, when you sit to meditate, your mind will throw a lot at you. Other days, your mind will be more settled. Either way, our practice is to be with whatever our experience is, bringing as much self-compassion and curiosity to it as we can.

Do remind yourself that it's early days for you in terms of the course.

When I focus on my breathing, I have a real problem finding a sensation at the tip of my nose…or, if I do, it is so fleeting that I can't keep track of it. I usually end up mentally meandering, either searching for something to pinpoint or just end up wasting time daydreaming and getting frustrated that I'm losing the point of the whole exercise.

Any suggestions?

It's not important where you locate the sensation of breathing. If it's not locatable at the tip of your nostrils, try focussing on the rising and falling of your belly as you breath in and out. Or even the sound of your breathing. No method is better than another. Just go with whatever feels easiest and most comfortable.

I've been practicing mindfulness for a full week now and have conflicting views on what to do when it comes to thoughts. One view is to just relax, observe them and let them pass. The other is to strive hard to focus but, when thoughts come, to just let them pass.

If I do the former, I tend to get lost in thought for the entire practice. If I do the latter, I tend to get frustrated. However, with the latter, I've heard that I should not be forcing anything...which leaves me confused! If I do not try and simply watch my thoughts pass whilst having a place to come back to such as my breath, I feel like nothing is being achieved and usually end up in a daydream which lasts the entire time I meditate.
Any ideas?

Striving hard is always going to be counterproductive.

Gently observe thoughts and let them pass, or 'self-liberate' as the Tibetans put it. That's the mindful way.

But if relaxation becomes the goal, mindfulness can easily become another form of striving.

Being mindful is opening ourselves to the present moment, being present in our own lives, not grasping at how we would prefer our lives to be right now.

It can seem very challenging at first.

Practice, practice, practice.

I have a long track record of becoming obsessed with things I get involved with – whether it is diets or relationships, whatever.

How can I stop myself becoming obsessed with mindfulness in the same way??

Be gentle with yourself - that's the most important thing here. If you find yourself thinking, 'What if I become obsessed with mindfulness?', treat that thought mindfully as you would any other thought. If the thought arises during formal meditation, simply notice the thought and return your attention to your anchor - breath, body etc.

Remember. You are not in competition with anyone.

Especially not yourself.

We're not trying to master anything here. Try to let go of any notions of success and failure. Be careful not to let mindfulness and meditation become new forms of striving for you. Keep your effort steady but don't overdo it.

This might sound a bit odd but I find myself crying a lot during meditation. When I still my mind and bring my attention to breathing or my body, I start to sob.
As I'm only on the first week, maybe this is a beginner's thing. Any ideas?

It's not uncommon for people to experience some challenges when coming to mindfulness. For many of us,

mindfulness is our first experience of sitting and facing what's going on in our lives, opening ourselves towards direct experience. That can sometimes be emotionally testing.

At this point in the course, simply be aware when you are crying. Try not to judge yourself for doing so. Let the tears fall and be aware they are falling. Simply accept that, in that moment, you are crying.

I read somewhere that mindfulness flattens emotions. What I think is meant by that is that meditation distances people from how they feel. I don't want this to happen. How can I avoid that?

A lot of ill-informed nonsense is written about mindfulness. Mindfulness practice does not flatten emotions in any way. It's not about distancing ourselves from emotions but being more aware of them as they arise.

Mindfulness is all about awareness. It's about paying attention and remembering to come home to ourselves, to our lives, in this moment. Mindfulness also involves acceptance, meaning that we pay attention to our thoughts

and feelings without judging them - without believing, for instance, that there's a 'right' or 'wrong' way to think or feel in a given moment. When we are present in our own lives, we are able to explore experience in a fresh, non-habitual way.

SESSION TWO: HONING AWARENESS

'Be attentive to inattention.' (Robert Powell)

'Joy is being willing for things to be as they are.' (Charlotte Joko Beck)

Theme For Session Two

In this second session of the course, we are looking to ground ourselves further in our bodies, our breathing and our awareness.
In the body part of the sitting/breath/body meditation from week one, we used parts of our bodies as anchors of attention.

Now, in week two, we are introduced to the body scan itself, in which you are invited to lie down and bring your attention to parts of the body over a longer period of time.

Secondly, we will practice a longer sitting/breathing meditation. In this meditation, we are invited to practice a kind of mini version of the body scan, simply noticing sensations in the body as we shift our attention up and down. As with the longer body scan, the idea is to simply

notice what is happening in the moment, without self-judgment.

Our aim in this course is to be more aware, more often. A powerful influence taking us away from being 'fully present' in each moment is our tendency to judge our experience in the moment as being not quite right in some way – that it is not what should be happening, not quite good enough, or not exactly what we wanted.

These judgments take us out of the actual experience of the moment and often lead us into a spiral of negative thinking where we lose sight of the possibility of choosing what to do next. In that sense, we lose the freedom to respond practically or wisely.

That freedom can be regained if we rest in awareness of what is happening inside us and outside us, rather than remain trapped in the cycle of self-judgment or wanting things to be other than they are.

'The range of what we think and do
is limited by what we fail to notice.
And because we fail to notice
there is little we can do
to change
until we notice
how failing to notice
shapes our thoughts and deeds.' (R.D. Laing)

The body scan provides an opportunity to practice simply bringing our direct attention to how things really are in the moment, rather than feeling that the moment that has already arrived should be some other kind of moment.

When we scan through our body, there is no goal as such. We are not looking for anything special to occur. We are not looking to change anything. We are simply paying attention to the sensations that are arising and falling away from moment to moment. In this way, we are able to rest in awareness. One way of thinking about it is that we are grounding ourselves in our bodies.

Turning Point: Pause to consider how infrequently you think about your body at all except when something is wrong with it.

For much of the time, we take our bodies for granted, completely unaware of how the body is feeling and what it is telling us about its wants and needs.

When we are in touch with what our body is telling us, we are in a position to respond wisely and fluidly rather than react impulsively and rigidly.

Our minds often wander off into the past or future, but our bodies are always in the present moment.

Being present in the body doesn't mean formulating ideas about it. When you bring your attention to sensations in the belly area during meditation, noticing how it expands and contracts when you breathe in and out. That's mindfulness in action.

Getting lost in harsh judgments about your body while you focus on your belly, that's not mindfulness. That's yet more unhelpful thinking.

Noticing that you are caught up in judgments about your body and how it ought to be, then gently bringing your attention back to your felt experience of sensations in the belly, that's mindfulness.

With practice, we learn to check in on our bodies regularly and listen to the messages it is sending us.

During the body scan you might occasionally fall asleep, lose concentration for long periods of time, or maybe find it difficult to feel anything in some parts of the body. This is not something to be concerned about. Those are all common occurrences, especially at this early stage of the practice. Try to accept that, whatever occurs during a body scan, that's simply your experience at that moment. Just be with that if you can, as best you can.

And remember that, when you are practicing the body scan, you are not in competition with anyone, including yourself.

This is not about striving for a certain kind of result. We're not trying to master anything here. Try to let go of any notions of success and failure. Be careful not to let

mindfulness and meditation become new forms of striving for you. Keep your effort steady but don't overdo it.

Mindfulness is process-oriented, not goal-oriented. It is not a means to a specific end.

If you talk to people whose day involves a run and ask them why they do it, most will not say that they run because it burns calories, strengthens bones or generates endorphins. They are more likely to say that running makes them feel better about their lives.

After completing this course, you might not spend too much time thinking about what percentage of your time your mind is running on auto-pilot or whether this week's meditation was 'better' than last week's. But you are very likely to feel better about your life overall.

With mindfulness, the invitation is to just be with the experience of paying attention.

Obviously, it is not possible to pay attention to everything all of the time. That would be overwhelming. Our brains have a limited capacity for working memory. There's only

so much our awareness can hold at any one time. So, mindfully, we bring a discriminating attention to one thing at a time.

When we notice our attention has wandered (drawn away by the ever-changing kaleidoscope of thoughts or external stimuli), we return to our chosen anchor. In this way we learn how to sustain attention.

From time to time, you will notice how mindfulness practice has re-shaped your life in so many ways. But it is important not to get hung up on the results or the pursuit of results. See these benefits as welcome by-products of sustained practice. And keep practicing.

Meanwhile, if you find yourself getting caught up in the pursuit of specific goals, be mindful about those thoughts. Observe them, let them go and remind yourself that mindfulness is about what is happening right now; it's not about what benefits might be there tomorrow.

What we are learning here is about accepting the moment as it is and not being attached to a specific outcome.

When we lie down for a body scan, is it possible to put to one side how we want to feel during and after? Because, if we attempt to manipulate our experience in this way, we are setting ourselves up for where we want to be, where we want to get to. The implication being that we are not OK where we are right now.

You might find yourself thinking, 'Why would I want to remain where I am if I'm feeling emotional distress or physical pain?' With mindfulness, we are invited to allow everything that is being experienced in the moment – pleasant, unpleasant, or something in between. We don't have to like it. The invitation is to accept that it is already here and attempting to push it away or ignore it is not likely to make it any better.

In the longer sitting/breathing meditation that is introduced in week two, we bring our attention to our breathing, noticing the in breath and the out breath. Not thinking about the breath. Simply tuning in to the breath in an open and receptive manner.

Breathing in, know that you are breathing in. Breathing out, know that you are breathing out. It's that simple.

If the mind has wandered, we register that fact and then, without getting caught up in the content of the thoughts, we let the thoughts naturally drift away without any judgment as we gently shift our attention back to the natural breeze-like flow of the breath. Allowing awareness of breathing to be at the foreground once again, as thoughts recede into the background. This might take a little getting used to and, again, patience is key.

In the early stages of meditation practice, it might come as a surprise just how busy your mind is, how continuous your thought stream is. It is important to remind yourself that it is not just your mind that behaves like this.

With practice, we become aware of just how quickly thoughts can arise, unbidden, and become overwhelming if we are unable to disidentify with their content, if we are unable to see thoughts purely as thoughts. Meditation teaches us to let go of thoughts and to see the difference between a situation and how we perceive that situation. We learn that any experience can be considered pleasant or unpleasant, depending on the situation in which it arises and the mental lens we view it with.

★

Turning point: Thinking is not the problem. However, how we relate to our thoughts can often be problematic. Thoughts possess no power of their own - they are just fleeting events. Their power rests entirely on the attention we bring to them.

We become absorbed in the story of our lives the way we become absorbed in a movie. There's no harm in watching a movie and losing ourselves in the dramatic ups and downs of the various characters.

When the hero dies at the end, we don't lose sleep over it. We might suspend disbelief for the duration of the film and lose ourselves in the twists and turns of the narrative but, when the credits roll, we are aware that we've been watching characters played by professional actors.

Often though, we forget that the mind is spinning us a story that can be as remote from actuality as any Hollywood movie. Furthermore, the way we interpret events often influences our feelings and determines our reactions more than the actual situation.

Imagine the following scenario. You attend the annual office party. Halfway through the evening, perhaps after a drink or two have been consumed, you spot Nigel from accounts across the room. You wave at him but he doesn't wave back. Instantly, your mind swarms with thoughts about the situation. Nigel obviously doesn't like me. I wonder how many people in the office don't like me? I never felt particularly liked at school. That's why I was so miserable as a teenager. Why is my life never easy? Why aren't I more likeable? Why…?

Consider how you would feel with all those thoughts racing through your mind?

Now consider the following scenario.

On the Monday following the party, when everybody has recovered from their stinking hangovers, you find yourself standing next to Nigel from accounts in the queue at the office canteen. Nigel seems friendly enough. The conversation turns to the party. Nigel mentions that he didn't particularly enjoy himself and you ask why. He tells you that he left his contact lenses at home and found it

difficult to see properly. 'I barely recognized people when they were right in front of me,' he laughs.

Consider how you would feel upon hearing this.

Turning point: Thoughts are not facts. So much of our suffering is caused not by what is actually happening to us but by the belief that what we are thinking is the truth. Mindfulness practice provides a release from this unconscious tyranny. With practice we are able to be mindful of thoughts as they happen, from moment to moment. We begin to see how thoughts colour our reality.

Our minds are naturally scattered. With thoughts running on auto-pilot, we veer from preoccupation with the past to preoccupation with the future, rarely showing up in the present moment.

If we wake up with thoughts about the vast potential of a spring day, those thoughts will affect the quality of that day. If we are consumed with fearful, anxious thoughts about

what might happen to us during the course of the day, that line of thinking will most likely impact on our experience.

Thoughts seem to have a life of their own, but you are not your thoughts. You may think continually but you are not your thinking any more than seeing means that you are an eye.

Thoughts are things you have, just as growing your hair is something that you do.

Think about this. If you are able to aware of your thoughts, then you cannot be your thoughts.

Your thoughts do not define you, as you might realize when you begin to be mindfully attentive towards the thinking process. When thoughts are held in awareness, they tend to lose their hold over us and so we are able to emerge from the trance of thinking.

There's an old story about a man on a horse, galloping at breakneck speed down a road. Another person, standing by the side of the road, shouts out, 'Hey! Where are you going?' 'I don't know,' comes the breathless reply, 'ask the horse!'

Like that wild horse, the mind is liable to rear up and gallop away at any time if we are not paying attention.
How many thoughts do we actually choose? If we pay close attention we might notice that most of our thoughts arise unbidden. In other words we don't choose them. They just happen. As the French physiologist Pierre Jean Georges Cabanis once remarked, 'The brain secretes thoughts as the liver secretes bile.'

But here's the good news.

You do not have to believe your thoughts. Rather than get hooked by them, you can choose to notice them and allow them to pass.

It is said that the average person has 76,500 thoughts a day. That's a lot of thinking. Some thoughts are useful and it pays to act on them. If you have a dentist appointment at 3pm today, you might want to think about getting ready in time so you don't miss it.

If somebody doesn't wave back at the office party and you find yourself thinking, 'Nobody likes me', it might be worth reminding yourself that thoughts aren't necessarily facts and

that some thoughts can be allowed to pass without believing in them.

In the forthcoming weeks we will learn to start noticing thoughts simply as thoughts, as passing mental events. We will learn that we can choose not to get caught up in their content and, instead, rest in spacious awareness.

We will also begin to see how thoughts, feelings and body sensations are interconnected.

With these realizations, thoughts tend to lose their magnetic charge. They come to be seen as passing neuroevents. Learning to hold our thoughts more lightly, we are more likely to move between them without feeling trapped or disconcerted. We learn to experience life without the overlay of the chattering mind.

Home practice for week following session two

Body Scan Meditation

Listen to the 25 minute or 40 minute Body Scan guided meditation on at least four of the next seven days. A helpful attitude to bring is letting go of any expectations and

judgments, just allowing your experience to be as it is, as it naturally unfolds. Use a notebook to record your experience each time you listen to the track. Also, make a note of anything that comes up during the week.

Sitting/Breath & Body Meditation

Listen to the ten minute Sitting/Breathing Meditation on six days out of the next seven. Give yourself one day off. Use a notebook to record your experience each time you listen to the track.

Mindful Activity

Choose one routine activity in your daily life and make a deliberate effort to bring moment-to-moment awareness to that activity each time you do it, just as we did in the raisin exercise. Possibilities include brushing your teeth, taking a shower, getting dressed, driving to work, shopping etc. Simply bring your attention to what you are doing as you are doing it.

NUTRITION - Week Two: Mindful Hydration

The rule of thumb is that humans can't survive without oxygen for longer than three minutes, without water for three days and without food for three weeks. This week, let's talk about hydration, number two on the list for survival after the air you breathe.

It is an inconvenient truth that we are two-thirds water and that pure, clean water is the cornerstone of good health. It's literally our most precious resource. Each cell in our body depends on water carrying nutrients and oxygen around the body, aiding in the digestion and absorption of food, the elimination of toxins and other wastes, regulating body temperature and blood circulation. It also cushions joints and protects tissues and organs from damage.

Did you know that even though water is readily "on tap" in the developed world, most of us are mildly dehydrated? Physical symptoms are headaches, fatigue, muscle cramps, increased heart rate and body temperature, and decreased perspiration and urination. The impact of even partial dehydration on our mental state includes impaired concentration, mental fatigue, loss of focus and increasing mental confusion.

The human brain is 85% water, and a mere 2% drop in our internal water supply can lead to problems with basic maths, short-term memory and focus. Not exactly what you seek when starting your mindfulness practice! Thinking of water as a precious life-giving and life-affirming treasure, we become mindful of its finite supply, our dependence upon our ecosphere and savour every sip (rather than glugging it down mindlessly), thankful for our continued access to clean drinking water.

In this country, water is so readily available, it's almost taken for granted. But although it covers 70% of the Earth's surface and is continuously regenerated through evaporation, 97% is salty seawater and 2% is frozen in polar ice caps and glaciers. Only a mere 1% of the world's water is usable water and much is already contaminated by toxic metals, chemicals and bacteria. As a novice 'mindful drinker' we should remember that, as our groundwater reserves become more depleted, clean fresh water is a finite resource and begin to think and act on water conservation issues. The UN predicts that billions of people will face severe shortages of fresh water by 2025 if we keep consuming and polluting our water at current rates.

Chronic dehydration has serious consequences, contributing to high blood pressure, headaches, poor immunity and digestive problems. As the body cannot maintain itself without water, a scarcity could cause a wide variety of diseases. However, our thirst mechanism is often mistaken for hunger and more often than not, we are dehydrated rather than hungry. A little mindful drinking can help with weight loss!

Drinking six to eight glasses of water between meals is thought to be sufficient under normal conditions. But bear in mind that the body's requirements for water are increased by heavy exercise, high temperatures or dehydrated, processed foods high in salt and sugar, and alcohol, of course.

Beware of taking health messages to extremes though, and start overdosing, as drinking excessive amounts of water in a short period of time causes the level of sodium in your blood to drop too low. This can lead to seizures and can even be fatal. If your urine is clear or straw-coloured, it's a good sign that you are well hydrated.

My 5 favourite water tips:

Add a slice of lemon or lime if you don't like the taste of water. Or add ice and a couple of strawberries.

Don't drink more than ½ glass of water with a meal as this dilutes your digestive juices, making it harder for you to digest your food. It's best to drink water in between meals. As an added bonus, you'll find that you tend to snack less!

Eating a healthy diet also helps to keep you well-hydrated. Fruit and vegetables contain plenty of water and the essential fatty acids in oily fish, nuts and seeds help our bodies hang on to and make use of the water that we do consume.

Avoid sugary fruit juices, squashes, and limit your consumption of caffeinated drinks and alcohol as these will dehydrate you.

Coconut water is great re-hydrant when exercising as it contains the same electrolyte level we have in our blood.

You won't find a better natural sports drink containing valuable nutrients, salts and sugars.

This week's exercise:

Keep track of what and how much you drink every day. If you drink less than six glasses of water (preferably filtered) or herbal teas every day, gradually increase your intake over the next week. Start with a glass first thing upon waking (before your first cuppa) and remember to drink in between or before meals. Slowly ease yourself into drinking more water and it will become a healthy habit for life!

'When we drink a glass of water, and if we know that we are drinking a glass of water, if we're concentrated on the fact that we are drinking water, mindfulness is already there. And the water drinking becomes deeper, truer, and real.' (Thich Nhat Hanh)

Jon's Reflections On Week Two

Reflections on the body scan

When my teacher casually announced that we were to do a body scan lasting between 30 and 40 minutes, I have to admit that my heart sank a little. Paying close attention to body parts over the course of a few minutes (during the sitting/breathing/body meditation), that was one thing. But 40 minutes? That's almost half a football match.

I struggled with it at first. The time spent focussing on my big toe of my left foot felt like an eternity. Then we moved to the little toe. And all the toes in between…

Then something happened. Some kind of turning point. I became curious about what was being felt in the sole of my foot, the ankle, the lower left leg…I began zoning on in the most subtle sensations in areas of my body that I hadn't been attentive to in years, and some I'd never given a moment's attention to in my whole life. I mean, who gives much attention on a daily basis to sensations felt in, say, the side of the right knee? I could now see the point of this. I was learning to respect what was happening in the moment,

to pay sustained attention without wanting anything special to happen, without wanting anything to change. I was learning to fully engage with my moment to moment experience. I was learning to simply be.

When I was on the nursery slopes with mindfulness, not every body scan was easy. Far from it. It took me a while to get used to the idea that every scan, as with any other meditation, would be different. Some days I found it easy to anchor myself by paying attention to specific body parts. Other days, my attention was all over the place. I learned to accept that this was my experience at that particular time and that all I needed to do was pay it the courtesy of gentle curiosity.

GERARD'S REFLECTIONS ON WEEK TWO

The Body Scan required a leap of faith for me, albeit one I was happy to make. It seemed an odd and pointless exercise at first, but once I'd got in the habit (and that was the leap), it repaid me in ways I hadn't imagined.

'To be aware, more often' as the course puts it.

Bringing awareness to any sensations in my toes was a challenging place to start. There was nothing there. Indeed, I'm not really sure I've ever felt anything in my toes during a body scan, much less between them. But the valuable lesson for me here was that it's not about feeling sensations - it's not about wanting the moment to be any different from it is. No sensation is just as fine as sensation. It's not about judging yourself or coming up to any standards. It's simply about noticing what is there and equally noticing, without judgment, if there is nothing there. This was a lesson I could apply to all sorts of areas in my life, and doing so played a major part in unclamping my head and helping me to relax.

Whilst relaxation is not the stated aim of meditation, I personally find it extremely relaxing most of the time. There are, of course, days when my brain never seems to slow down at all, but I figure they are the days I need it most of all. Even when I'm constantly and monotonously bringing myself back from distraction, I notice that my body has stayed still throughout, which feels vaguely revolutionary. The course points out - and this was another big turning point for me, "when you are practicing the body scan, you are not in competition with anyone, including yourself."

The idea that not everything in life has to be goal-oriented seems anathema in the West and increasingly in the East. The realisation that, at least while I am meditating, I can free myself of all this pressure, was profound for me. It wasn't long before it started seeping into the rest of my life just as profoundly. Results as welcome by-products rather than do-or-die pressure points.

The Body Scan had some knock-on effects. Whilst meditating on the bus (which became a regular habit on my 30 minute journey from my home in Lewes to my Brighton workplace), I would find it increasingly easy to sink in to awareness of my body. As well as anchoring me in the present moment, this served to make me aware of just how bad my posture usually was when I sat on a bus seat, almost comically so.

Mainly though, it seemed that every time I became deliberately aware of my body, I was automatically back in the present. It was a quick and easy way of grounding myself, particularly if I noticed that I was drifting off into a stream of negative thinking.

FAQ FOR WEEK TWO

I want to ask about paying attention. When exactly do we pay attention? Say, for example, if we are trying to give up smoking with the help of mindfulness. Is it when we light the cigarette or before?

Maybe think of 'undoing' a habit in terms of before, during and after; exercising present-moment awareness at those three distinct times:

Before: You can form the intention of being mindful when the next urge to smoke arises.

During: You can pay attention and choose to be open to the urge, craving or difficult feeling that typically spurs the habitual behaviour, gently focussing on that feeling and allowing it to come and go rather than engaging in the habit.

After: If you engaged the habit, you can consciously extend yourself kindness and forgiveness, rather than compounding an unhealthy habit with negative judgments or harsh self-criticism.

I am in the second week of the course and feeling less anxious already.
One thing about thoughts though.
I use thoughts to make plans, whether it's making shopping lists or planning a visit to the dentist.
Nothing wrong with those thoughts, right?
What about making plans to make myself safe? For example, if I miss the last night bus and have to walk home through a dodgy area?
How can I be mindful about those kind of thoughts?

Thoughts are not the problem. How we relate to thoughts can be problematic, especially if we get too attached to their content.
Many thoughts about the future arise from worry and fear.

As human beings, we are natural problem-solvers but it is easy to get confused between doing something practical in order to address an issue and worrying about it obsessively.

These thoughts can be so powerful that, when we have the thought, it's as though we're actually experiencing the catastrophe. Whereas it's only a thought - it's mere speculation.

It is these kinds of thoughts that bring an awful lot of suffering.
It is these thoughts that we learn to be mindful about.

With time and practice we learn to be discerning about thoughts. Some are worth acting on. Most are mental chatter that serve no purpose other than to make us feel fearful and dissatisfied.

As for plans, they are an unavoidable part of daily life. However, we need to be careful not to get too attached to outcome.

When it comes to personal safety, simply take the appropriate precautions. There's a big difference between planning a safe route home and getting caught up in frantic worry about what might happen on your journey.

I'm struggling a little to understand what 'being on auto-pilot' actually means. Any help would be appreciated.

Planes have a button called automatic pilot. When pilots push that button, they don't have to consciously control the aircraft - the plane flies by itself.

People can also run on auto-pilot and that's not always a bad thing. Once something has become automatic, you don't need to consciously think about it again and can give your attention to something else. Auto-pilot also saves some energy. Imagine if you had to think about every movement of your body when you were driving or walking, activities that involve hundreds of muscles; thinking in this way would be exhausting.

Operating on auto-pilot may be OK in certain circumstances but, if your whole life is run automatically, you are likely to miss what's going on around you. Your mind thinks the same old thoughts, you may react unnecessarily when things don't go your way, and your stress is compounded without you being fully aware of this process.

Our minds wander about 50% of the time, but every time we practise being mindful, we are exercising our attention 'muscle' and becoming mentally 'fitter'. We can actively choose to be more focussed in our attention rather than passively allowing our attention to be dominated by that which distresses us and takes us away from the present moment.

Does anyone have experience in practising mindfulness when exercising, jogging, working out or taking part in sports?
How does that work?

We can practice mindfulness whilst doing pretty much anything, including exercising, working out or taking part in sports.

But it could be argued that, if we are immersed in those activities, then there's little need to bring mindfulness practice in as an extra element, as it were.

When you cycle, just cycle. And don't wobble!

When meditating, sitting up in a chair is not comfortable for me. I've even tried propping up the back legs so the chair itself is more flat. But I just can't get comfortable. It's like I'm trying too hard to keep my posture 'as it

should be.'

On a meditation bench with a cushion is also not comfortable.
Lying in bed, sitting up - this has been the most comfortable for me. But is it an accepted posture for meditation?

The sitting positions that most teachers advise for meditation (lotus, straight-back chair, meditation bench) are mainly chosen for ease of breathing. Also, in those positions, there's less chance of slouching.

But most teachers would also say that, from the point of view of self-compassion, your physical comfort is the prime concern.

Given that, lying in bed/sitting up would not be inadvisable in any way and ought not to devalue the meditation.

Ultimately, you can choose whatever position you like. Be open to experimentation. You might find that different postures result in different degrees of comfort, and also make for varying meditative experiences.

What does noticing one's thoughts mean? For example, I get carried away by thinking and then come back to mindfulness. What do I do with that thought? For me it comes down to either ignoring it completely and accepting that I am mindful again, or letting it control me. I cannot mindfully see where the thought goes.

Also, because the illusion of the self is strongly connected with mindfulness, at least in my perspective, I sometimes feel like I am suppressing my thoughts. What do I do to stop this?

In mindfulness practice, we begin to notice that thoughts are discrete mental events. That is, they arise and pass by. Perhaps more importantly, by noticing the temporal nature of one's thoughts, one can begin to question whether they are true or not.

Often, when we are anxious or depressed, it's largely because we believe our thoughts to be truths or facts (rather than passing phenomenon). Often, our sense of reality is bent out of shape by our thinking, by our opinions about how life is, and how it should be.

In mindfulness, we notice the thought and let it go. In formal meditation we would return to the anchor (usually the breath) after noticing that the mind has wandered. Invariably, the thought ebbs away once it has been noticed. But see if this is your experience.

For the time being, at least at this stage of the course, it might be advisable to put questions about the illusion of self to one side, as it will only confuse matters. The question of 'self' is addressed in later weeks of this course.

This might sound like a daft question but I'm getting confused as to how I should be breathing during meditation. I guess I've never really thought about breathing before. It's just happened. Now I'm beginning to tie myself up in knots about it.

Assuredly, there are no 'daft' questions about mindfulness, at this stage or at any other stage.

All questions are valid.

There are quite a few approaches to breathing in meditation. With mindfulness, you are generally instructed not to try to control the breath or force it in any way.

However, when we bring our attention to the breath, there is sometimes a tendency to change it in some way, usually rather subtly. As much as possible, allow the breath to do its own thing. Just let it be.

As you breathe out, simply let the breath exit the body. And as you breathe in, similarly, let the breath simply enter the body.

Remember, this is about being with breathing and not thinking about breathing. If thoughts arise around the breathing, just notice this, then bring the attention back to the breath. Think of your breath as your home base, a place you are always welcome to return to, both during formal meditation and in your everyday life.

Above all, don't worry too much about getting everything 'right' at this early stage. Most of this stuff falls naturally into place after a few weeks.

When I sit to meditate I sometimes start feeling overwhelmed with all the sensations that are being felt. This becomes very unsettling.
Any advice?

That's not an uncommon reaction during the early stages of meditation practice.

Patience is key here. As you continue your practice, it's highly likely that this problem will subside.

For the time being, make it your intention to keep coming back to your anchor. In a sitting/breathing meditation, when you start feeling overwhelmed with sensations, focus your attention as much as possible on the breath. During a body scan, come back to the part of the body appropriate in that moment.

During meditation I'm finding that I can anchor myself well to the breath, but it's not so easy when I'm at work. I'm employed at a busy estate agents. It's a stressful occupation and my boss is something of a difficult character.

I've tried coming back to the breath when I get anxious at work but there's always something new that needs doing. More houses to sell and let, more impossible demands from my boss…
Any advice?

When you're in a busy workplace, your attention pulled hither and thither, it can be challenging to bring your attention to the breath or any other anchor.

In those situations, it may be easier to bring your attention to your posture and adjust it accordingly.

Also, week three of the course introduces the three-minute breathing space which is designed to help people take a pause during the day so that it's possible to be less reactive and more responsive in stressful situations. So watch out for that meditation.

I think I'm getting along OK with this course. I'm now in the second week and starting to see a few benefits.
However, I do get consumed with thoughts that I am somehow doing it wrong and not progressing.
Can you help with that question??

?

Your situation is not uncommon. In our culture, we're under pressure to get things right all the time from an early age.

Just follow the course as closely as you can and, if possible, keep the intention of doing your home practice. You will probably find that thoughts about 'doing it wrong' gradually drop away.

Also, do remind yourself that the thought 'I am somehow doing it wrong and not progressing' is just a thought. It's not a fact. Thoughts, all thoughts, possess no power of their own. Their power rests entirely on the attention we bring to them. We become absorbed in the story of our lives the way we become absorbed in a movie. We forget that the mind is telling us a story that isn't necessarily true.

Notice the thought and gently let it go.

I'm really enjoying the course so far and feeling much better in myself.
My question is: what is the best way to remind myself to be mindful during the day?

There are numerous apps available which act as prompts during the day to remind you to bring your attention back into the present moment.

However, regular practice should do the job by itself. In other words, with practice, we naturally begin to notice when we are not being mindful and act accordingly - bringing our attention to our experience right now.

Patience is key.

Stick with it if you can.

With practice, we learn to fold mindfulness into our daily lives so that being mindful becomes second nature. We learn to be fully awake in our daily lives without striving in any way.

Is it recommended for a practitioner of mindfulness to avoid drinking coffee, before or after meditation?

Not an easy one to answer as coffee affects people in all kinds of ways.

?

But there should be no harm in having a coffee before meditation so long as it's not affecting your practice in any way. If you notice that you are jittery, for example, just notice that. And maybe notice the difference when you refrain from drinking a cup before meditation.

Personal experimentation is the fastest route to making the right call on this and, indeed, many other things.

One thing I don't understand about coming back to the moment...what if I don't like this moment? Wouldn't I be better off seeking something better in the present moment than enduring something unpleasant?

The present moment is already here. We don't have to like it, only accept that is has arrived, just as it is. But, if we attempt to escape from it or deny it, we are denying our experience in that moment.
Any thoughts of seeking something better in the present are really about seeking something better in the future, even if that future refers to the next ten seconds.

Mindfulness teaches us to accept what is already here. If we are in a difficult situation, we can begin to change our circumstances. But we cannot change what is already here.

Mindfulness invites us to simply be with our experience in this moment, to be aware of what we are thinking and feeling, seeing and touching etc.

It is important to bear in mind that accepting the moment as we find it does not equate with passive resignation.
We can recognize that, within spacious awareness, we actually have a choice. We might choose to take decisive action. In some situations the wisest course of action might be to do nothing - or simply wait.

When negative thoughts arise (during meditation or in everyday life) I have begun tricking myself into thinking about something happy rather than about something miserable or depressing. It seems to be working too.
Does this sit OK with mindfulness?

With mindfulness, we are not looking to change our thoughts.

We are simply noticing thoughts as they arise and accepting that they have arisen. From the standpoint of mindfulness, attempting to turn negative thoughts into positive thoughts is another form of avoidance.

Try simply noticing the thoughts without getting caught up in their content, then gently bring your attention back to your anchor (the breath, or parts of the body during a scan).

I am the sort of person who gets bored very easily. You might say I'm the hyperactive type. That's one reason why I thought I'd give mindfulness practice a try.

I have just finished week two. I find the body scan very boring and notice my mind wandering off left, right and centre. My mind wants to do anything but focus on my kneecap or my elbow. I keep thinking, 'What is the point of all this?'

But I don't want to give up just yet. When I'm not meditating I'm starting to notice that I'm less hyper than usual. So maybe it's working. I just wish the body scan wasn't so BORING!
Any advice??

Don't worry. A little bit of boredom is not uncommon at this early stage of the course.

We have a tendency to fight boredom as though it was our enemy. Like any other thought or feeling, boredom is fleeting. It comes and it goes. It's a natural part of life.

As this 8-week course develops you will see what happens when you turn towards that feeling of boredom and become interested in it as part of your present moment experience. 'Oh, that's interesting, I'm bored' can become a natural response that you meet without resistance.

Similarly, if you find yourself impatient for a meditation to finish, you can simply be curious about that.

Remember. When we meditate, we sit with whatever arises in the moment: euphoria, depression, delight, irritation, boredom, fascination…We don't meditate as a kind of insurance policy against times in the future when life gets challenging. We meditate to be with what is - good, bad and neutral.

SESSION THREE: THE BREATHING SPACE

'Breathe, and let be.' (Jon Kabat-Zinn)

'Confront the difficult while it is still easy; accomplish the great task by a series of small acts.' (Lao Tzu)

Theme For Session Three

In this third session of the course, we explore ways of folding our mindfulness practice into our everyday life.

It is important to remember that mindfulness is not a matter of how well we meditate in a chair or on a cushion. Mindfulness is not about 'chilling'. It is about zoning in rather than zoning out.

It is about how we live our lives. From day to day. From moment to moment.

Turning point: In a very real sense, mindfulness practice is what we do when we sit down to meditate, lie down to do a body scan or do some mindful movement. And the rest of the day is the meditation. In that sense, meditation is a result of the practice.

Every moment of the day is an invitation to drop into present-moment awareness, tune into your experience and adopt a much broader perspective on any situation you find yourself in.

Mindfulness can include everything that you do. Absolutely everything. Any routine activity, even tying your shoelaces or combing your hair, can be made into a mindfulness practice when you bring your full attention to it.

In any situation, from sitting in the dentist chair to queuing at the supermarket check-out, we can rest in awareness of the present moment, become fully aware of what we are experiencing, rather than be overwhelmed by thoughts, feelings and body sensations.

Even in the midst of our most trying moments, when we imagine the weight of the world on our shoulders, we will know how to locate the still point where we feel centered and steady, aligned with what is.

This way freedom lies. The freedom of realising that we have a choice in the way we respond in the moment, realising that we don't have to be a victim of our own destructive habits, realising that we don't need to be a

prisoner of circumstances. And from this, a deep and profound contentedness can spring. In time, life can feel more like running downhill than trudging uphill.

'I would love to live
Like a river flows
Carried by the surprise
Of its own unfolding.' (John O'Donohue)

One of the main features of the third session is the introduction of the three-minute breathing space. This is a kind of mini-meditation but it ought not to be regarded as an alternative to the longer sitting meditations you've already been introduced to on this course.

Rather, it is to be regarded as an important meditation in its own right.

The three-minute breathing space offers a spacious, non-judgmental way to reconnect with the present moment, and to your immediate experience.

In formal meditation, it usually lasts three minutes but the beauty of the breathing space is that it is easily adaptable to

suit any situation you find yourself in. It can be any length you choose, even as little as ten seconds.

It is especially useful when life is at its most frantic and demanding.

On average, a person breathes 22,000 cycles of breath per day. Each of those breaths is an invitation to connect to the present moment.

Just as the breath itself is always available to you as way of anchoring yourself in the moment, so the breathing space is always at your disposal should you need to drop into it.

The three stages of the breathing space (awareness, gathering, expanding) are designed to cultivate meditative awareness.

When we rest in awareness, we are able to anchor ourselves so that we are able to face the next moment more calmly, more openly and with greater clarity. We can begin to accept the moment just as it is without impulsively or unconsciously reacting to it.

If you are quick enough, you can sometimes catch the reaction as it is arising and turn it into a wiser, more creative response instead.

By simply taking a breath or taking a breathing space, we might be able to see that we don't need to add to the problem we apparently face by panicking or over-thinking it. By pausing in this way, by being present, by freeing ourselves from reactivity, we might just be able to see the situation more clearly.

It's all in the noticing.

It's all about being aware.

As the course progresses we will expand the possibilities of what can be met in the field of awareness during formal meditation and in our everyday lives.

Let us remember. When we sit down or lie down to meditate, we are invited to set aside any definite ideas of how we want to feel during and after. The invitation is to accept that this moment is already here and attempting to push it away or ignore it is not likely to make it any better.

When we push our thoughts, feelings and body sensations away we are denying ourselves the opportunity to know life as it is and have an intimate relationship with our own experience.

If you are beginning to grasp some of this, then you are starting to own the practice. You are beginning to open up to the vast possibilities of mindfulness practice and apply it to your everyday life. You have begun to give yourself back to yourself – a most precious gift. You have begun a journey which will help you to navigate life, in all its beauty and sorrow, more skilfully. You have begun a love affair with yourself.

If none of that has occurred yet, don't worry. It is still early days.

Again, mindfulness requires intention, practice, and patience. But it can also be fun and should never be a chore.

Keep practicing, and go easy on yourself.

Home practice for week following session three

Three minute breathing space

Listen to this guided meditation twice a day on six days out of the next seven. Record any impressions on a sheet of paper each time you listen to the track.

Twenty minute breath/body/sounds/thoughts meditation

Listen to this guided meditation on at least four of the next seven days. Use a notebook to record your experience.

Mindful Activity

Choose one routine activity in your daily life and make a deliberate effort to bring moment-to-moment awareness to that activity each time you do it, just as we did in the raisin exercise.

Possibilities include brushing your teeth, taking a shower, getting dressed, driving to work, shopping etc. Simply bring your kind attention to what you are doing as you are doing it.

NUTRITION - Week Three: Mindfulness Before Meals

Digestion already begins with the sight and smell of food. We start salivating before meals when they look and smell tasty… This is the nervous system sending messages to the gut that food is on the way, and to get ready by producing gastric juices and digestive enzymes to break it down into smaller components. You can actively support the digestive process by spending a minute appreciating your meal before eating: look at it, admire it, smell it – your gut will thank you!

Chewing your food is the mechanical process of grinding it all up. In addition, we produce around a litre and a half of saliva per day. Saliva contains an enzyme that breaks starchy food like bread or potatoes into smaller units. When we start chewing, signals are sent down to the stomach to produce the right concentration of gastric juices, depending on what's in your mouth.

If you take time over your food and enjoy it, your sense of taste is enhanced. People with hurried eating habits, who literally "inhale" their food whilst in the middle of other activities, do themselves no favours. They are inviting chronic digestive and a host of other health problems.

It has to be said that current lifestyles do invite careless eating. Think about the term 'fast' food. When you are in a restaurant that provides fast food, you are meant to eat fast food fast. You are not there to take time over your food but get on with it and make room for the next customer. Most fast food is also soft food, easy to swallow quickly, and so encourages us to be lazy about chewing habits. As a result, we are prone to overeating and bolting down our food without a thought as to whether we have chewed properly or our stomach has had time to produce enough gastric juice to process the meal. Fast food may well be 'ready to eat' but are we ready to eat it?

Gastric acid is strong stuff: it helps to sterilise food and reduce our exposure to nasty bugs. In addition, the acid frees minerals such as calcium, iron and zinc from our food – this is an important first step towards preventing anaemia or osteoporosis. Gastric acid is also crucial for the digestion of protein, and it stimulates the pancreas to secrete enzymes, and the gallbladder to release bile.

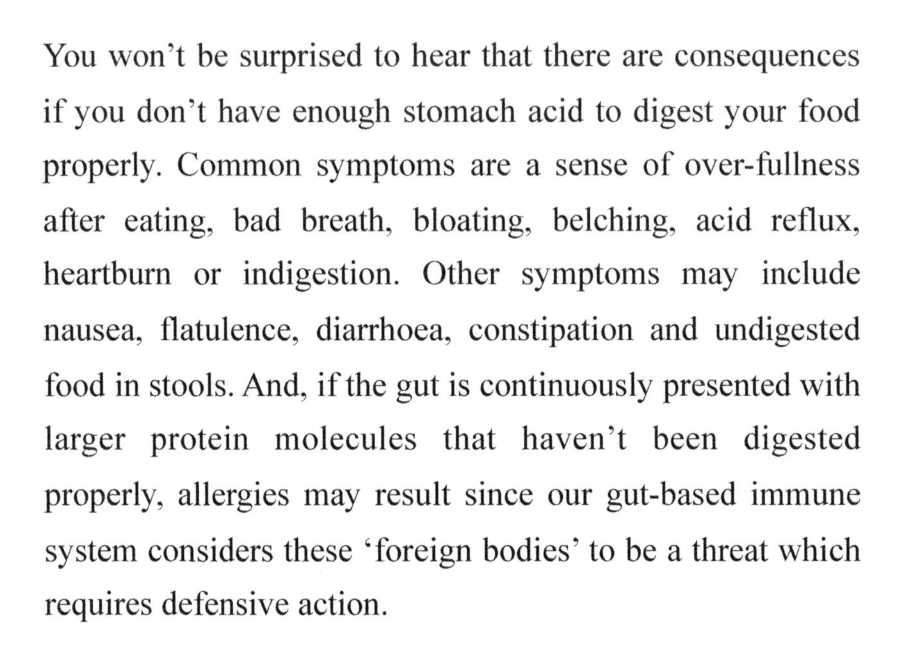

You won't be surprised to hear that there are consequences if you don't have enough stomach acid to digest your food properly. Common symptoms are a sense of over-fullness after eating, bad breath, bloating, belching, acid reflux, heartburn or indigestion. Other symptoms may include nausea, flatulence, diarrhoea, constipation and undigested food in stools. And, if the gut is continuously presented with larger protein molecules that haven't been digested properly, allergies may result since our gut-based immune system considers these 'foreign bodies' to be a threat which requires defensive action.

People with heartburn or acid reflux often mistakenly believe they suffer from excessive stomach acid and rely on indigestion remedies. But they may not realise that these medicines, which promise only short-term relief, act to reduce already low acid levels even further, disrupting the entire digestive process, often making digestive problems worse long-term.

Imagine that your body is a sophisticated recycling plant: we chew and chomp and grind our food (hopefully), add digestive juices and process it into tiny particles which can then be reassembled into new parts by the body or excreted as waste. As mentioned before, it's not just important what you eat, but what you manage to digest and absorb from your food.

If something goes wrong in your factory - let's say your food hasn't been ground up properly or hasn't produced enough gastric acid and digestive enzymes. Consequently, less nutrients are absorbed and large, undigested food particles can disturb our delicate internal 'machinery', potentially even affecting the workings of the brain. All the more reason to take your time before eating, while eating and to chew, chew, chew …

Exercise:

A Three Minute (or One Minute!) Breathing Space is an ideal practice before each main meal. It gets your body into the "rest and digest mode" and acts as a good incentive to relax, eat slowly and chew your food thoroughly. If necessary, remind yourself to do this by sticking a post-it note or card on your dining table. Notice how you feel after eating.

'At home, reserve a time for dinner. Turn off the TV; put away the newspapers, magazines, mail and homework. If you are eating with others, work together to help prepare dinner. Each of you can help with washing the vegetables, cooking or setting the table. When all the food is on the table, sit down and practice conscious breathing a few times to bring your body and mind together, and recover yourselves from a hard day's work. Be fully present for each other, and for the food in front of you.' (Thich Nhat Hanh)

Jon's Reflections On Week Three

Reflections on the three minute breathing space

When I first learned about the three-minute breathing space, I'll admit to a feeling of some relief, knowing that there were shorter meditations available. Quickly though, I came to realize that this was anything but a conveniently brief substitute for longer meditations and found it fairly easy to drop into my day - between phone calls or while I was waiting for food to cook.

Pretty soon it seemed completely natural for me to do a shorter version throughout the day. I found it useful in the kind of situations that I tended to find quite stressful. Standing in an overcrowded tube carriage, I could practice a breathing space rather than allow myself to feel overwhelmed by claustrophobia, impatience and frustration. Realising I could drop the meditation into my day at any point and that it could be any length I chose, I appreciated the ready availability of it. Sitting, standing or lying down, it was a great way to ground me in the moment.

I now see it as an invaluable part of my growing mindfulness repertoire, alongside longer meditations.

Reflections on the breath/body/sounds/thoughts meditation.

It was during the third week of my first course that I realized I was becoming more interested in myself. Not in a navel-gazing, ego-driven way. But in a way that helped me relate to myself with greater curiosity and alertness, rather than allowing myself to be defined and constrained by conceptual judgments and narrative spin.

This meditation alerted me to the fact that breath isn't the only anchor we can rely on to bring ourselves back into the present.

Pretty much anything can be used to anchor us in the moment.

The idea of sound as an anchor particularly captivated me. As far back as I can remember, I've always been hypersensitive to sound. Loud noises would trigger irritation. My anxiety levels would soar if I attempted to have a conversation in a crowded bar due to my inability to

filter out background noise. At times, I would find the noise of everyday day pretty much unbearable.

Learning to meditate on sounds has helped me to relate to sounds in a different way. When a sound is annoying to me – like when a neighbour's music is turned up a little too loud, I'm able to notice my annoyance and let it go. If I'm travelling on the bus and find myself irked by fellow passengers bellowing into their smartphones, I find that I can use my attention like a mindful lens, zooming in on the voices and becoming curious about the rhythms and timbres of individual voices, or zooming out and hearing those voices as part of a broader soundscape – which might include the pneumatic 'tss' of the bus braking, my own breathing, sounds on the street outside…Suddenly, the sound of teenagers loudly arguing about the respective merits of Candy Crush Soda Saga and Candy Crush Jelly Saga is no longer annoying. It just is.

I continue to struggle with conversations in noisy public places but I have found a mindful remedy for that. If I'm having trouble hearing what someone is saying, I simply suggest we move to somewhere quieter and continue the conversation there.

In this meditation, I particularly liked the way the focus segued from sounds to thoughts. I was particularly engaged by the idea that most thoughts, much like sounds, are not of our choosing. Somewhat mysteriously, they arise and then they ebb away. As with sounds, we don't need to react to thoughts. We can actually choose not to be drawn into their content and be consumed by them.
Bringing greater attention to my experience in the moment, I learned to relate to my thoughts and feelings in a more skilful, responsive way rather than react from them. I began to see my life situation in a clearer context and from a wider perspective, experiencing a much greater sense of freedom and flexibility in my everyday life.

This is possible for anyone who commits to a more mindful way of life. With practice, we build resilience to help us manage life when it throws up difficult challenges. Living mindfully, we learn to trust our responses. Our thoughts and actions are brought into closer alignment with our most profound needs and our most authentic values. We connect with what we truly are.

GERARD'S REFLECTIONS ON WEEK THREE

The idea that mindfulness is something we fold into everyday life is something I completely missed before the Turning Point course. Knowing that the three-minute breathing space (or less in emergencies) is available any time I need it has increased my confidence walking into any and every situation.

For me, this is what turns mindfulness from a hobby into a way of life.

I think of it a bit like going to the gym. The meditation is like the exercise you do at the gym, but the rest of the day is when you truly benefit. And like the gym, it takes a while to really reap the full benefits. I think of returning from distraction like a muscle that gets a bit stronger every time I notice my mind has wandered. Thinking of it like that has been a great help on those days when the mind doesn't stop wandering for the duration of a meditation.

During this course, I found myself increasingly training my focus on one sound at a time - no more talking over the telly, for instance. The mute button now gets hit every time I have a conversation.

Mindful eating, as discussed by Martina in the week 3 nutrition section, is a massive challenge to me. 54 years of conditioning and bad habits sometimes take a while to break down. This in turn calls for a lot of self-compassion when I 'wander', which is often.

So many times in life, I've seen the common sense in a way of behaving, only to behave in the opposite way. Deeper urges, instant gratification urges - problems I'm still chipping away at - lose some of their power when I look at myself with compassion rather than self-criticism.

On a positive note from an unexpected source, my time-keeping has become far better as mindfulness changes my relationship with time. No longer scared by unhelpful concepts of 'wasting' time, I now get to meetings early and simply enjoy the moment, either meditating or just being, as I wait for the appointed time to come around.

No more stress about late buses, no more clock-watching. Enjoying the moment has enabled me to get out of the loop of always striving impatiently for the next moment. This on its own is a massive stress-buster.

FAQ FOR WEEK THREE

Occasionally, my back hurts when I meditate. As I understand it, I shouldn't react. Instead, I should remain still.
But why shouldn't I react if I'm feeling uncomfortable? Why can't I just shift my posture so that I'm comfortable again?

Nobody is suggesting that we sit through pain even when it becomes unbearable. Instead, bring curiosity and patience to the discomfort. Maybe, after a few seconds, the discomfort will ease or dissolve completely. Even for that second or two, can we be curious and/or patient? Can we live with a little discomfort?

What happens if we don't immediately react to it? See for yourself.

If the discomfort persists, try adjusting your posture. If that doesn't work, perhaps it's best to stop the meditation and try another time.

I'm into week three of your mindfulness course and it really does seem to be bringing me some benefits. I

completely get the idea of creating space around things like thoughts and feelings. I feel like I'm getting less overwhelmed by situations, which was the main reason I came here in the first place.

One thing though. I seem to find it impossible to ever meditate in complete silence. I tend to use my front room and invariably there's traffic rumbling past, cars beeping horns, the sound of pedestrians talking, etc.

I guess silence is very important as far as meditation goes. So I feel like I'm not meditating properly if there's always the distraction of noise.

Try to remember that, when we meditate, we are not looking to create a situation of sensory deprivation. Finding anywhere that offers complete silence is increasingly challenging in this increasingly frantic world and not at all necessary – we are looking to be a part of the world, not apart from it.

You might find that the more you react to the noise, the more it will bother you.

When you are distracted by noise, simply notice that you have been distracted and return to your anchor (the breath etc.)
Or, if you happen to be practicing a sound meditation, incorporate the noise into the practice. It is equally possible to meditate on the sound of a car horn as a bird singing.

When I move from sound to thought in the meditation of week three, am I being invited to go through my thoughts or simply look on them with mindful attention?

We're simply bringing awareness to our experience in the moment. So the question of 'going through' thoughts does not arise. We are simply noticing our thoughts as they happen without being drawn into their content. We neither cling to them, nor repel them. We are learning to experience life without the distracting overlay of the chattering mind.
And remember. You don't have to act on your thoughts. You don't even have to believe them to be true.

I don't understand the non-striving/non-goal aspect of mindfulness. Surely the goal is to feel better about life? No?

Almost everything we do in life we do for a purpose, to get something or somewhere. In meditation, this attitude can be a real obstacle. That is because, in respect of goals, meditation is different from all other human activities.

Ultimately, it has no goal other than for you to be yourself, simply to be in the present moment. To enable this, no striving is necessary. Seeing this may point you toward a new way of relating to yourself, one in which you are trying less and being more.

When we give up all this resistance to the present moment, we often find ourselves feeling better about life. So much of the pain and pressure we feel in situations arises from our resistance to what is, rather than the situation itself. As we learn to stop entering this world of unmindful resistance, we are naturally regaining our energy, our mind and our sense of life just as it is.

We begin to see that, in each moment, things are as they are, and they cannot be any different.

Moment by moment, we use mindfulness to help us return to just this – without the obscuring overlays created by our

judgments, criticisms and ideals. Each moment is an invitation to awaken to the moment.

I can't believe the difference this course has made to me in three short weeks. I'm finding that the meditations are getting calmer and calmer; also, I seem much calmer in my everyday life. As a long-term anxiety sufferer, this new-found sense of calm, even serenity, is something of a revelation to me.

Would it be too optimistic of me to expect things to continue on an upward curve? Or, at least, can I expect this sense of calm to remain?

Be careful not to turn 'being calm in the present moment' into a fixed goal. Awareness of what is doesn't mean that we attempt to manipulate experience to feel a certain way. Besides, that has never been shown to work.

A common mistake made by mindfulness practitioners with anxiety issues is to expect to achieve states of calm through meditation. This is a form of grasping - a seeking to indulge in pleasant states and to avoid the unpleasant. A wiser orientation would be to appreciate calm states when they do

arise and to treat more turbulent states with acceptance and self-compassion.

A greater sense of calm is often a welcome by-product of regular practice but we don't meditate to feel calm. Think of meditation more as a way of checking in on what your experience is right now, a way of reconnecting with yourself, a way of fully participating in the moment.

Am I right in thinking that mindfulness is about changing who we are? If not, what would be the point?

Yes and no. Mindfulness practice might well bring about change but that's not why we meditate. Mindfulness is less about striving for change and more about the freedom to simply be with the experience of the moment. With practice, we learn to notice and let go of habitual patterns, remaining in the awareness of whatever life is presenting to us in the moment.

Over time, we might realize that we don't need to cling to our destructive habits; we don't need to constantly try to be elsewhere; we don't need to strive to live up to someone else's idea of who we should be.

In these ways, change is highly possible. But that's very different from meditating with a specific goal in mind.

Can you how you're supposed to watch your thoughts go by (rather than try to repress them)?
If I'm thinking the thought, then I can't simultaneously be watching it. And once I have caught my mind wandering like this, I can't watch the thought because I'm no longer thinking it. All I seem able to do is to gently stop the thought and go back to watching the breath.
Metaphors like watching thoughts as if they're flowing past in a river, or going past like cars observed from the side of a motorway don't seem achievable to me.

If those metaphors don't work for you, that's fine. Don't worry about that. Either drop them, come up with some of your own or dispense with metaphors entirely. They are not compulsory.

Regarding your first question, is it possible to consider those passing thoughts as being held in awareness rather than thinking about thinking? With mindfulness, we are learning to hold our thoughts more lightly, moving freely

between them without getting snagged up in them. It takes practice. And patience.

For example, a thought comes up during meditation:
'I must remember to phone Emily after I finish meditating.'

The temptation is to cling onto this thought, lest you forget the phone call. The panicking mind might feel quite stringent about this, particularly if there could be further negative consequences of forgetting the call.

The trying-too-hard meditator may think all the above in a split second and then try to push the thought away and rush back to the breath. Perhaps tinged with the slightest guilt that yet another thought has distracted them, and the hope that the next one won't happen along for a while.

The mindful response is to note the thought, without judgment, simply as a mental event occurring in the present moment. Once noted, the thought will naturally shift to the side of the stage (as all thoughts do) whilst the mindful person gently attends to the matter at hand.

(?)

I thought I was doing OK in the first two weeks of the course but the wheels seem to have come off in this third week. I've been really slack with the home practice and, while I haven't lost faith in the idea that mindfulness could be very beneficial for me, I can't really see right now how I'm going to get back into it.

It's not uncommon for people to hit the wall in practice, particularly during the first few weeks of an eight-week course.
The important thing is to be kind to yourself right now. You haven't failed. It's just that – in your mind - your practice has somewhat stalled.

Perhaps leave it for a few days and return to the very start of the course, bringing beginner's mind to each day's practice, noticing any tendency to want your meditations to be a certain way.

Also, perhaps considering making your meditation time more pleasurable – a bit of self-pampering never hurt anyone. Have a bath before you start. Treat yourself to something you really like after finishing a meditation. Start

looking at meditation as the beautiful act of self-love that it is.

I'm into the third week of the course now and definitely feeling more mindful in my everyday life. Maybe only 5% more mindful but it's a start, right? I guess the ultimate aim is to be 100% mindful? That's to say, mindful every waking moment. I can imagine how chilled out that would feel!

The aim is not to be mindful every moment of the day. That would be a wholly unrealistic goal.
Most of us probably spend about 90% of our time in our heads and 10% in our senses or our bodies. We don't need to aim to reverse this ratio. Even a 50/50 ratio may be an unrealistic goal. And anyway, who's counting? The true measure is simply how we feel, beyond all mathematics.

We can aim to be a little more mindful as we go along, as our practice deepens and evolves. But it helps to let go of percentages and specific aims. That's not what mindfulness is about.

Nor is this about achieving perfection, an impossible aim built on endless striving. A meditator who aims for perfection is bound to meet disappointment. Like life itself, meditation is guaranteed to deliver a mixed bag of experiences.

Go easy on yourself. Self-compassion is key, every step of the way.

I'm getting on OK with the course. I like the way it is presented and it is easy to follow.

But I'm confused about one thing. I'm not hearing much about feeling more positive. Isn't that what being mindful is all about??
Shouldn't I be trying to redirect my awareness away from that feeling of negativity to be able to feel more positive about stuff?

There are practices which cultivate that approach. But mindfulness isn't one of them.

Mindfulness is about being with what is - good, bad or indifferent. It's not about trying to evade negative thoughts

or unpleasant feelings. It's not about wishing that this moment was any different. It's about accepting that the moment has already arrived, and meeting it with an open heart.

When difficult thoughts or emotions arise, we have a tendency to try to push them away, or distract ourselves from them. But this rarely succeeds. When you push a thought 'away', it doesn't go anywhere, nor does it disappear. It simply buries itself deeper inside you, like a tick, feeding on you until it resurfaces, often in a more dramatic manner.

In noticing thoughts, leaning in towards them, we are less likely to get stuck in habitual patterns. This way freedom lies. The mindful awareness of the difficult is the beginning of its dissipation.

Can I be mindful towards any anxious, angry and depressive thoughts or feelings that frequent my mind and, at the same time, let my mind roam free, without any control being exerted on it?

In a way, mindfulness works two ways. We can be deliberately and purposefully mindful, say when we set out on a nice country walk and we decide that we're going to be mindful on the journey, appreciating the beauty of the trees and so on. But mindfulness is as much about catching ourselves when we're not being mindful.

Say, if we're halfway through a country walk and realise that we've not noticed the trees or anything else as our heads have been full of thoughts about tax returns and what Boris said to us at the meeting last week. In that second instance, just the act of noticing brings us back into the moment.

One of the first things you learn about mindfulness is that you are not your thoughts. Further to that, we realise that some thoughts are useful and some are destructive/pointless etc. Within that, there's a choice – we are giving ourself more options and, as a result, the chance to act more skilfully.

We will choose to act on some thoughts such as making a meeting on time. Other thoughts (ruminations on the past, dark-hued speculations about the future) we might choose

to see purely as thoughts and watch them dissolve, as it were, using the mindfulness skills we have learned.

It's worth asking oneself how many of our daily thoughts are actually of any real use.

In any case, there's always a choice and the choice comes at the moment of awareness when we become aware of our thought stream. The choice comes in the space that we create between the thought and our response to it.

So, yes, you can be mindful towards any anxious, angry and depressive thoughts or feelings that frequent your mind and at the same time let your mind roam free, without any control being exerted on it. Or, perhaps more accurately, you have the choice as to whether you want to be mindful about a particular thought or whether you want your imagination to run wild. The choice is yours at the very moment that the thought occurs.

The key point here is that this is not about controlling thoughts. It's about being gently aware and letting go. In that awareness we find the space in which to respond.

I'm getting a little confused about thoughts. I know we're not trying to stop thinking. But some thoughts are useful, right? Is it a case of allowing the useful thoughts in and heading the non-useful thoughts off at the pass?

It's more a case of discerning which thoughts are useful (and acting on them if that's appropriate) and which thoughts simply need to be acknowledged and allowed to pass.

In formal meditation, notice the thought (whether it's a harsh judgment or a non-emotional memory) and come back to the breath, or whatever anchor you are using.

Outside of formal meditation, we are able to discriminate between thoughts we need to act on (such as 'I must remember to send a birthday card to my brother' or 'My tooth is hurting – I need to make an appointment with my dentist'), harmless nostalgic memories (perhaps hearing a song and remembering where we were when we first heard it) and negative spirals of thought.

All are thoughts and we learn to see them purely as thoughts. Some we act on, some we enjoy while they last,

some we observe as they arise and fall away.

Practical thoughts generally don't cause us problems. It's the third category of thoughts, the negative spirals, that tend to be the 'stickiest'. But we aren't trying to get rid of those thoughts. We are learning to allow them to be by relating to them differently than before.

I've been doing the course for three weeks now. I like it and I think I'm beginning to understand how mindfulness works.
But I still feel anxious. I want my anxiety to go away real bad. Is this the wrong way to be thinking?

It's natural at the start to expect quick results from mindfulness. We have either read great things about the practice or people we know have told us how transformative it's been in their lives. But this is about your experience, not somebody else's. Generally, comparisons with others are not useful.

Also, most of us come to mindfulness because we want something to change in our lives - we want to feel less

anxious, less depressed…we want to feel less pain…

With patience and self-compassion, we come to see that mindfulness isn't about quick fixes, nor is it actually about getting anywhere. It's about being with what is. The way we're feeling right now, right in this moment, that feeling has already arrived. Whether it's pleasant or unpleasant, it's already here. We can't change the moment that's already arrived. But a good deal of our lives seems to be spent wishing away the present moment, wishing for an entirely different moment.

As Pema Chodron says, 'Meditation is not about getting out of ourselves or achieving something better. It's about getting in touch with what you already are.'

Getting in touch with what we already are - that's what this is all about.

It's a wonderful adventure. But it takes patience.

Be gentle on yourself and take your time.

SESSION FOUR: MEDITATION IN MOTION

'For a plant to grow well, you have to water it a little every day. If you just pour a bucket of water on it once a month, it will likely die between waterings. The same applies to meditations.' (Matthieu Ricard)

'In meditation we return to where we already are – this shifting, changing, ever-present now.' (Steve Hagen)

Theme For Session Four

In this fourth session of the course, we look at ways of anchoring our awareness in the moment while our bodies are in motion - through mindful movement (a kind of light yoga) and walking meditation. Just like the breath, the body is your anchor, your support and stability, available whenever you need it.

Think of these exercises as meditation in motion.

While practicing mindful movement we are discovering the edges of our physical capabilities while bringing awareness to our breathing and bodily sensations.

Effectively, we are learning to listen more closely to what our bodies are telling us from moment to moment.

It is important to approach these mindful movements with an attitude of non-striving. The emphasis is on gentleness and kindly listening to our bodies - working towards but not beyond what feels difficult. Go easy on yourself.

With practice we learn that these exercises offer yet another way of connecting to our present moment experience, another way of waking us up to each moment.

Most of us don't normally associate meditation with the movement of the body.

When newspapers and magazines select a photograph to illustrate a piece about any kind of meditation, they invariably choose an image that denotes absolute stillness.

Not a little misleadingly, the photo will usually depict someone (typically, a beautiful, scantily clad woman or a Brad Pitt lookalike in dharma pants) sitting in a state of absolute bliss in the full lotus position in front of a perfect sunset, usually somewhere distant and exotic like Goa.

The implication being that you not only need to be a particular type of person to meditate, you also need to wear certain types of clothing, find the perfect location, sit cross-legged no matter how uncomfortable that might be for you, and remain utterly still.

All nonsense, of course, up to and including the bit about needing to be completely motionless.

Turning point: The invitation to be mindful in our everyday life applies just as much when we are in motion as when we are sitting or lying in quiet stillness. We can use our bodies as a tool for heightening awareness. We can learn to be in the body as we walk, as we turn and reach for something, as we prepare to sit down or stand up.

Practicing bringing your attention back to the body again and again gives you the key to expanding your awareness

from times of formal meditation to living mindfully in the everyday world.

'Walk out
Like someone suddenly born into colour
Do it now.' (Rumi)

Walking meditation is another way of bringing awareness into our daily lives. This simply means bringing our attention to the direct experience of walking as we are taking each step. Knowing we are walking as we are walking.

Usually, when we walk, we are concerned only with getting from A to B. All too often, for many of us, the walk is all about the destination, all about the getting there, the earlier the better.

Wrapped up in ruminations about the past or worries about the future, we might not notice anything that's happening around us for the entire duration of the walk.

When we walk mindfully, we fully arrive with each step, waking up out of auto-pilot and becoming attentive to our

present moment experience. We can notice the sensations and movement of our feet, legs, arms, head and body as we take each step. We can notice our breathing. Undoubtedly, thoughts will intrude, but we can just notice them, and then bring our attention back to our walking.

Home practice for week following session four

Three minute breathing space

Listen to this guided meditation once a day on six days out of the next seven. Use a notebook to record your experience.

Mindful movement (sitting)/Mindful movement (standing)/Walking meditation

Alternate these meditations through the week so that you practice each of them twice, allowing yourself one day off in seven.

When practicing mindful movements or walking meditations, it is important to work within your own physical constraints at all times.

If you find any of these exercises too challenging, please feel free to adapt them to suit your own needs.

If your fitness and flexibility are limited in any way, take it easy, progressively enhancing your range of movement.

If you are in any doubt about your capabilities, you might like to discuss these exercises with your doctor, specialist or physiotherapist.

If you don't have any physical concerns, try to strike a balance between pushing yourself too far and not stretching far enough.

This tends to come with practice, as you build up the muscles of awareness.

And don't be too concerned about doing these exercises 'perfectly'. If you find the instructions hard to follow at times, just practice the meditation as well as you can. The important thing here is attention and awareness, not expert precision.

Mindful Activity

Choose one routine activity in your daily life and make a deliberate, conscious effort to bring moment-to-moment awareness to that activity each time you do it, just as we did in the raisin exercise. Possibilities include brushing your

teeth, taking a shower, getting dressed, driving to work, shopping etc. Simply bring your kind attention to what you are doing as you are doing it.

NUTRITION - Week Four: Minding Your Microbiome

This week, let's talk about the microbiome, a collection of around 100 trillion bacteria living happily in and on our body, mostly residing in our gut. According to the latest research, they even inhabit the brain. These bacteria are critical for our overall health and wellbeing, and in particular, our mental health.

The microbiome consists of an incredibly complex ecosystem of bacteria that have a vital role in the digestion and absorption of food. But these bacteria are also intricately involved in immunity, detoxification, skin health, hormonal balance, weight loss – and mood and brain function. Our thoughts, our motivations and emotions, our abilities and ultimately our actions relate in complex ways to the health of the microbiome.

The number and diversity of these tiny microorganisms are influenced primarily by our diet, our genetics and our lifestyle. We naturally acquire normal bacterial flora at birth and during the first two years of life, and it helps to prime our immune system and provide greater resistance to disease. Increasingly, this delicate microbial ecology is threatened by poor eating habits and a diet unnaturally high in sugar and refined carbohydrates, processed foods and artificial sweeteners. Many other factors also deplete the microbiome, including infections, antibiotics, stress, oral contraceptives, chlorinated water and environmental pollutants.

So, is there anything we can do to replenish our rapidly dwindling stores of beneficial bacteria?

In the early 20th century, the Russian immunologist Dr Elie Metchnikoff realised the value of beneficial strains of bacteria in fermented milk products. Fermentation is the ancient and economical art of preserving food through the action of lactic acid bacteria, yeasts and their enzymes.

Fermented foods are easy to digest, nutritious and have long been associated with significant health benefits. Dr Metchnikoff certainly believed that the longevity of the Bulgarians was mainly due to their high consumption of yoghurt.

Nowadays, commercially produced "live" yoghurt or liquid yoghurt-type drinks may not be potent enough to restore gut ecology. It all depends on what type of "live" organisms have been used, whether they have been heat-treated (and therefore destroyed!) and how they have been stored. Some bestselling brands add processed fruit, sugar, colours, flavours, artificial binders and fillers to their yogurts. The most beneficial is plain "live" organic yoghurt and it only takes a minute to stir in your own fresh fruit for taste.

Another fermented milk product, Kefir, originated in Eastern Europe. Traditionally, Kefir was made by adding the culture to camel's milk. Any milk alternative can be used, if you don't happen to have a camel to hand - including milk from cows, goats, sheep, buffalo - or from milk substitutes such as soya, seeds or nuts.

Like yoghurt, Kefir contains probiotics, so-called 'friendly' bacteria, which are responsible for keeping our intestines healthy and disease-resistant. Whereas yoghurt contains transient short-lived beneficial bacteria, the 'friendly' bacteria in Kefir appear to be more resilient at colonizing the human gut and staying 'put'.

Fermented vegetables have also long been important sources of nourishment. Archaeologists have discovered that fermented plant foods were first consumed by prehistoric hunter gatherers.

One of the most well-known is salted, fermented cabbage, known as sauerkraut (see recipe below). Apart from its tangy flavour, sauerkraut offers remarkable health benefits, such as improving digestion. The fibre and lactic acid bacteria in sauerkraut facilitate the breakdown of proteins and promote the growth of healthy bowel flora, protecting against constipation and diseases of the digestive tract.

It is important to introduce any fermented food or drink gradually, with just a small amount daily and to build up your intake slowly to let your gut flora adjust. Commercially available fermented products are generally pasteurized and lack friendly bacterial cultures, and may even contain vinegar to make the sauerkraut appear fermented.

To experience the delicious taste and health benefits of real sauerkraut, check out brands in health food stores or on-line

– or you can always just make it yourself, just like our hardy ancestors did…

Exercise:

To promote optimal digestion and absorption of nutrients, try eating live yoghurt or Kefir every day, or eat a little sauerkraut before or with every meal, especially later in the day with heavier meals. If you have digestive problems drink a few tablespoons of sauerkraut juice daily.

Always remember that stress has a damaging effect on the microbiome – we all know that we first experience acute stress 'in our gut', or we sense a 'gut feeling' that something is wrong - and that to maintain and improve gut function, we need to keep this stress under control. Practising mindfulness engages the relaxation response, which in turn makes your gut bacteria happy and ultimately keeps YOU happy!

Home-made Sauerkraut Recipe

Ingredients

1 shredded cabbage

10 juniper berries (optional)

1 tsp caraway seeds (optional)

1-2 tsp non-iodized pickling salt

1 cup of filtered water mixed with 1 tsp non-iodized salt

Method

In a sterile glass jar or stoneware crock, mix cabbage, juniper berries, caraway seeds and salt. Packing a bit into the jar at a time and pressing down hard with a wooden mallet helps to force water out of the cabbage. The salt draws juice out of the cabbage and the resulting 'brine' allows the cabbage to ferment gently.

Add filtered, or non-chlorinated, salty water (1 teaspoon salt per cup of warm water) up to the rim of the jar.

Using a small plate (or lid) which is about 1cm smaller in diameter than your container and a weight (a large stone will do), weigh down the cabbage to keep it under the liquid and cap loosely with a lid. Place the jar on a tray to catch overflowing juices.

Keep jar between 60°F to 70°F for 1-3 weeks. The fermentation process will take longer in cooler weather or a cooler room. Check the container regularly and top off with salty water if the level falls below rim. When ready, skim any (harmless) mould from the top, close the jar tightly and store it in the fridge.

Jon's Reflections On Week Four

Reflections on mindful movement and mindful walking

When I first practiced mindful movement (standing), I started to wonder what this had to do with mindfulness. Then I started noticing the difference that even the tiniest of movements made. Just lifting my arm a little had a big effect on my breath and the rest of my body. Then the judgmental thoughts began to drop away. A few minutes in and I realized I was not only seeing the benefits, I was actually enjoying the practice.

Mindful walking was even more of a revelation for me. On my first 8-week mindfulness course, my teacher led a walking meditation around the spacious yoga room we were gathered in and I got the first inkling of just how infrequently I'd been present when taking walks in the past. This struck home more forcibly the following afternoon when I took an hour-long walk along the rolling chalk downland and dry valleys of the South Downs, near my home in Brighton.

I reminded myself that I would be walking more slowly than usual, taking easy steps, aiming to be present and alert with every step, paying close attention to what was happening in my body, from moment to moment.

At first, my mind frequently wandered off and I found myself lost in the usual preoccupations with past and future, absorbed in all too familiar stories about my life along with all the self-criticising, brooding, worrying, speculating, prattling, judging – all of it colouring and re-shaping my direct experience in the moment.

Then I'd catch myself and gently lead my attention back to the immediate sensations of my feet touching and lifting off from the ground, the slight stretch of my thigh muscles as I took each step, the movement of my hips…

Each time I noticed my mind had wandered and tuned in to what was actually happening in my immediate experience, it felt like I was riding the swell of the moment, welcoming life as it presented itself, meeting it whole-heartedly and engaging with it.

It then occurred to me that I had a choice in this: a choice, in any moment, as to whether to be at the mercy of automatic thinking or whether to be awake to my own experience, fully present to the glorious scenery around me, the company of my dog or anything else that deserved my careful, loving attention.

I'd always enjoyed walking. But I started to realize how infrequently I'd been present during walks. My body might have been somewhere between A and B on my journey, but my mind was invariably somewhere else, hopelessly scattered, lost in the rabbit hole of thinking. Endlessly distracted by the free-wheeling kaleidoscope of thoughts, I had noticed so little on thrice daily walks with my dog that it mattered little whether I was ambling along the South Downs on a beautiful spring day or walking through a city centre car-park in winter drizzle.

I began to dawn on me that we've never really walked until we've walked mindfully, giving our full attention to the moment, knowing that infinite moments of beauty, joy and surprise are waiting to be found if only we look and listen.

GERARD'S REFLECTIONS ON WEEK FOUR

Walking down the local High Street here in Lewes (East Sussex, UK), I spent so much time in my head, oblivious to pretty much everything except the auto-pilot that got me across roads safely and ensured I didn't bump into other people. It's a beautiful high street, full of delightful little shops and caressed by beautiful green hills and valleys on the horizon. Always visible but seldom seen and less appreciated when my brain was elsewhere all the time.

Mindfully walking along, I'm now aware of my body - of where the strains are in my legs and back as I walk. Of the tap tap tap of my feet as they make contact with the pavement. As this method brings me into my body, it brings me into the present and suddenly I notice all the beauty that is surrounding me.

I notice the people on the other end of the dog lead where before I only ever noticed the dogs (our mindful role models). I look up sometimes where I only used to look ahead, and see all kinds of things not seen before.

In time, I got rid of my car. You don't have to do this, obviously, but I did. No more road rage, no more tiring trips on the motorway, no more car-related bills. Instead I get the bus or the train. This way, I feel more connected to people. I am blessed with the opportunity to smile at the bus driver and my fellow passengers. To commit random acts of kindness when the opportunities present themselves.

Waiting for the bus is no longer an issue as I'm not longer waiting. I'm doing whatever I'm doing until the bus arrives. If it's late, no matter. Spending that time in 'the now' makes it far more pleasurable for me, whatever the weather.

I often do body scans on the bus, which has the effect of making long journeys a good thing. It's about the journey now, rather than hurrying to the destination. The now, not the future.

There are some seats on the bus that face sideways, rather than the usual forward/backward positions. I love those, a great reminder that it's about the moment right now, not how long I've been on the bus or how long until I get off. As the song says, give up yourself unto the moment, the time is now.

FAQ FOR WEEK FOUR

I've heard mention of 'The Seven Attitudes of Mindfulness'. What are they?

These are the seven attitudinal foundations of mindful practice that constitute the major pillars of mindfulness practice.

They are as follows:

Non-judging: Not getting caught up in our ideas and opinions, likes and dislikes.

Patience: An understanding and acceptance that sometimes things must unfold in their own time.

Beginner's Mind: Seeing things with fresh eyes, with a clear and uncluttered mind.

Trust: Trusting in your intuition and your own authority.

Non-striving: Trying less and being more.

Acceptance: Coming to terms with things as they are.

Letting Go: Letting our experience be what it is.

I've always been a worrier. A lot of my worries involve comparing myself to others and feeling I come up short - eg. how much money I have, how successful I am, how attractive I am to the opposite sex...
Do you think that most people suffer from worrying in some way? Or am I just the over-sensitive, over-thinking type?

I'd say it's a fair bet that most people, certainly in the western world, live worried lives. We are taught, nay encouraged, to do so.

But worries are just thoughts.

We can't live by comparing our own lives with the lives of others. Besides, speculating about how happy or miserable other people might be is just another thought, another concept, yet another thing that takes us away from the moment that we could be living.

?

When we sit and meditate for the first time, we become aware of just how frantic our minds are. Mindfulness teaches us to relate to our thoughts in a different, healthier way. We begin to see that thoughts have no actual solidity or substance. It's pure mental chatter, the mind just doing what the mind does.

It takes practice and it takes commitment. It needs to become a part of your life. It won't be hurried and striving for results will become counter-productive.

This applies to worry as much as anything else. As you have probably found, pushing worries away does not get rid of them. In mindfulness, we are learning to be with them, lean in to them and let them go.

It takes time. So keep practicing and be kind to yourself. Remember, worrying is often a form of self-harm disguised as self-protection.

OK. I'm throwing this one out there.
Which creature is more mindful? Cat or dog?!!!!!!

Great question!

?

The Brighton Mindfulness Centre team have put their heads together on this one.

We're not sure which is more mindful but we do know this:

Treat a dog well and feed it daily. The dog will regard you as the centre of the universe.

Treat a cat well and feed it daily. The cat will regard itself as the centre of the universe.

I'm enjoying the mindful movement exercises but I don't see what they have to do with meditation. It feels more like yoga to me. Or am I missing something?

There are some similarities with yoga. But perhaps think of mindful movement as using your body as a way to awareness. Practicing bringing your attention back to the body again and again gives you the key to expanding your awareness from times of formal meditation to living mindfully in the world.

Think of it as mindfulness in motion.

Ultimately, of course, 'mindfulness' and 'yoga' are just labels, just words we use as shortcuts. So I wouldn't worry too much about how any given practice is labelled, as long as it helps.

What do you do about itching? Now and again I have an intense itch, a feeling like beetles crawling into my body. It only lasts for a few seconds but it really gets to me. When I'm doing a guided meditation I am so distracted by this that I have to scratch it. Is there any better way of dealing with itching?

The next time it happens, simply be aware of the itching. Bring your curiosity to it. If it becomes too much, then scratch it. You are not ruining a meditation by giving in to the itch.

I'm getting a lot out of the Turning Point course but I'm becoming slightly anxious about what meditation is likely to bring up for me. I had quite a troubled background and years of therapy haven't helped me exorcise the 'ghosts' from the past. Are there any areas of my life that mindfulness will not 'reach'?

Mindfulness practice can entail a fair amount of courage. It takes courage to sit with difficult thoughts about the past and the feelings that these thoughts generate.

This doesn't mean that we have to throw ourselves in at the deep end when we are not ready. Be gentle and kind to yourself. Mindfulness keeps its own hours and will not be hurried.

In later weeks of the course, you will be invited to turn towards difficulty. That is the time to test the waters properly.

SESSION FIVE: LOVING-KINDNESS

'Through meditation practice we learn to enter into silence, and there the fruits of the practice reveal themselves: wisdom, which is seeing deeply into the true nature of life, and compassion, the trembling of the heart in response to suffering.

Wisdom reveals that we are all part of a whole, and compassion tells us that we can never really stand apart.

Through this prism we see life with openness, knowing our oneness. We find wisdom and compassion coming to life, transforming how we understand ourselves and how we understand our world.'
(Sharon Salzberg)

'A human being is part of the whole, called by us Universe, a part limited in time and space. He experiences himself, his thoughts and feelings as something separated from the rest – a kind of optical delusion of his consciousness. This delusion is a kind of prison for us, restricting us to our personal desires and to affection for a few persons nearest to us.

Our task must be to free ourselves from this prison by widening our circle of compassion to embrace all living creatures and the whole nature in its beauty. Nobody is able to achieve this completely, but the striving for such achievement is in itself a part of the liberation and a foundation for inner security.' (Albert Einstein)

Theme For Session Five

In this fifth session of the course, we explore ways of cultivating both self-compassion and compassion for others.

Along with attention or awareness, the quality of compassion is one of the central pillars of mindfulness practice.

Loving-kindness is intricately woven into mindfulness. In fact, mindfulness could quite accurately be defined as compassionate attention or compassionate awareness.

Removing compassion from mindfulness would be akin to removing wetness from water.

It cannot be done.

Loving-kindness is the glue which holds all of our mindfulness practice together because greater compassion for both ourselves and others is the most revolutionary and transforming reward we can offer ourselves. Beginning a meditation practice is a strange and challenging thing for many people. Filling it with compassion is how it becomes an ongoing, beautiful experience - a love affair with yourself. Loving-kindness fosters a gentle intimacy with all aspects of life that you may not have experienced for years, maybe since childhood.

Turning point: With compassion, we can undo our long-held habits and approach our own suffering and that of others with a more generous, more open, more tender, more receptive, more patient, more tolerant, more empathic heart.

If we are able to be kind to ourselves, then there is no obstacle to opening our hearts and minds to others. It rewards both ways. As author Mary Anne Radmacher writes, 'As we light a path for others, we naturally light our own way.'

When we stop judging and begin to accept ourselves for who we are, we can begin the process of accepting others for who they are. That process begins with self-acceptance and opens a pathway to empathy and compassion for all beings. Along the way we have the opportunity to learn about the true nature of friendship, love, acceptance and forgiveness.

This is all solidly based on scientific evidence.

Time after time, scientific research has shown that cultivating self-compassion leads to greater feelings of wellbeing.

As well as boosting self-compassion, mindfulness practice makes us more likely to help someone in need and increases activity in neural networks involved in understanding the suffering of others and responding appropriately.

Leading authorities on self-compassion have shown that self-compassion is more beneficial than self-esteem to our psychological wellbeing. Self-compassion cultivates 'greater emotional resilience, more accurate self-concepts, more caring relationship behavior, as well as less narcissism and reactive anger.

When we are compassionate, when we experience loving-kindness, when we see how interconnected we all are, we are able to see that every one of us shares the same wish to be healthy and content, to be in touch with our wholeness, to transcend fear and despair.
We see that our own stories are always intrinsically interwoven with those of others. We do not need to feel alienated and disconnected. We do not live in isolation.

The clothes we wear, the food we eat, the appliances we rely upon…as Martin Luther King once said, 'Before we even walk out of our door in the morning we are already indebted to half of the world.'

Living with more compassionate awareness, it becomes easier for us to unhook ourselves from past slights, real and

imagined, so that we are able to devote more time and energy to what is truly nourishing and worthwhile in life. In effect we make a conscious choice to end suffering rather than prolong suffering. We learn to stop feeding the voices of disdain, judgment, blame and mistrust.

Put simply, loving-kindness is a strong wish to allow love, generosity, contentment, understanding, forgiveness, peace and ease of being into one's life, and to wish the same for others. It is a gentle and balanced commitment to kindness and openness.

'Of the good in you I can speak, but not of the evil.
For what is evil but good tortured by its own hunger and thirst?
Verily when good is hungry it seeks food even in dark caves, and when it thirsts it drinks even of dead waters.'
(Kahlil Gibran)

With loving-kindness, we may open to the idea that the displeasing behaviour of others is rooted in their own pain and unsated desires. If we can stop the kneejerk reaction of judging another, we can look deeper into their situation, or at least realise they have their reasons, no matter how unreasonable they appear to be.

We may even come to think that, if we'd had their DNA and their same life experiences, that may have been the way we would behave in that situation.

To do this is not to be passive, nor does it excuse bad behaviour or suggest we should allow the unallowable. It is simply introducing less judgment and more compassion into your everyday life. The first winner in this situation is you.

In loving-kindness meditation, using plain, uncomplicated language, we begin by wishing compassion for ourselves.

Then, with each stage of the meditation, the ripples of compassion spread out to others, eventually to include all living creatures. At each stage we bring an open curiosity to our immediate responses - in terms of thought, emotion and body sensation.

There is no textbook ‘correct’ response to be found here. As with other areas of mindfulness practice, there is no goal to aim for here, no special state to strive for. The idea is to simply be with whatever is arising in the moment.

The cultivation of loving-kindness is for the benefit of all. For the benefit of ourselves, those we love, those we have struggles with, and total strangers. It can be all-inclusive. It can be unconditional. It can be boundless.

It is important to remember that, as with all other meditations and exercises on the course, loving-kindness is invitational and all stages of it are strictly optional.

For some people, a certain amount of resistance comes up during loving-kindness meditation, particularly when they are invited to wish ease of being on someone that they have a problem or an issue with.
With good reason you are invited, at that stage of the meditation, to choose someone who is not necessarily your biggest enemy or someone you have a long-standing grievance with. Instead, you are invited to choose someone like a work colleague who you currently have a slight difference of opinion with, or a family matter you need to resolve some issue with.

You might feel the urge to, as it were, jump in at the deep end.

But the clear invitation is to gently, tentatively, test the waters by choosing someone at the lighter end of the 'problem' spectrum to wish ease of being upon.

Always be gentle and kind to yourself.

Make compassion rather than fear or blame your default position.

Be compassionate in thought, speech and action.

Start each day with the intention to cultivate kindness.

Choose not to add to the harshness of the world.

Yes, the world is full of suffering, but it is also full of the overcoming of suffering.

Let your decision to engage with loving-kindness be your turning point. The moment when compassion starts to win out.

Compassion and forgiveness do not always come easy.

Sometimes they provide us with our greatest challenges. How can we show compassion for those who have caused us great hurt? How can we forgive those who have left a trail of emotional devastation in their wake, causing pain to us and those we hold dearest? Sometimes, being compassionate takes great courage, firm commitment and enormous perseverance.

Remember. Loving-kindness is not a demand. It is a benign invitation.

Let us pose it as a question: Is it possible to wish ease of being on someone who may have wronged us in the past?

This does not mean that we have to condone the unacceptable and harmful. Only that we don't need to cling to enmity and the need for sour recrimination all our lives. Even if we cannot bring ourselves to forgive a particular person, can we mindfully offer the slightest gesture of understanding their way?

Just how much is possible here?

Loving-kindness doesn't necessarily entail agreeing with the way someone is behaving or condoning it.

Being compassionate doesn't mean that we can't establish clear boundaries. Even if we need to keep our distance or even walk out of someone's life completely, it doesn't mean that we need to do so in an unkind fashion. We might even find it in us to gently explain to the other person why we are taking that course of action

If we dwell on the negativity of others, we only get eaten up with feelings of bitterness and blame.

How long do we need to hold on to the hurt and hate? How long are we prepared to allow feelings rooted in the past to spoil the present?

Are we willing to start undoing our toxic patterns of aversion, resentment, envy and blame?

Are we ready for the healing to begin?

We do not have to like the difficult stuff that arises in all our lives from time to time. But we can be less resistant to it and even befriend it.

That befriending does not begin and end with formal meditation.

The real challenge is to take this befriending of difficulties into our everyday lives and all the encounters that take place during the day.

Rather than get impatient with the confused old lady in front of you in the supermarket check-out queue as she searches for her money-off coupons, is it possible to wish her ease of being?

When our neighbour ignores us in the street yet again, can we give him the benefit of the doubt, perhaps see that he might be struggling and suffering, that he wants to be loved, accepted and valued just like the rest of us? And can we wish happiness for him? Right now.

When our work colleague is being 'impossible' yet again, can we accept for a moment that there may be reasons why

this person sometimes behaves the way they do, and wish them freedom from harm?

Or can we see that our negative feelings towards them are based on a small fragment of who they are, and it is this that we have mistaken for the whole? Can we acknowledge that we need not pile our own suffering on top of theirs?

When we pass a homeless person and find ourselves judging ('Why can't they find a job? Why can't they at least make an effort?'), can we pause to consider that we don't know the first thing about that person's life story, that we have no idea what has brought them to this place, put them in this unenviable situation?

Did they choose to be where they are now?

Can we find compassion for them?

Can we find time to help them in some small way?

Even if it is only a kind word.

When our parent/partner/child is not behaving exactly as we would wish them to behave at a given moment, is it possible to wish that they be safe and sound. Right in the firm jaw of events, even when it's easier to lose control and get cross with them?

That person who wronged you all those years ago? The one you can't forget or forgive? The one that makes your blood boil when you think of them? Is it time to let go? Is it possible to wish them well, wherever they are in the world? Can we allow that he or she is deserving of compassion? After all, it is your blood boiling, not theirs.

Again, this is an invitation, not a demand.

Doesn't this person suffer pain, loss and disappointment just like you and all the rest of us? Doesn't this person, like you and me, want to feel at home in the world? Perhaps this person is the one in the most pain? Isn't this person going to get sick, get old and eventually die? Is this person really so different from you, or me?

Is it possible for us to step back for a moment and appreciate that none of us is perfect? To take a transitional,

mindful pause and ask ourselves, 'What would be the caring thing to do right now?

Compassion is where true healing begins.

There's an old Zen story about two monks which is pertinent here.

The two monks are walking from one village to another and they come upon a young girl sitting on the bank of a river, crying.
The older monk approaches her and says, 'Sister, what are you crying about?'

She says, "You see that house over there across the river? I came over this morning early and had no trouble wading across but now the river has swollen and I can't get back. There is no boat.'
'Oh,' says the monk, 'that is no problem at all,' and, after asking for her permission, he picks her up, carries her across the river and leaves her on the other side.

The two monks continue their walk in silence.

After a couple of hours, the younger monk can stand it no more.

'Brother,' he says, 'as monks, we have taken a vow never to touch a woman. What you have done is a terrible sin. You ought to feel thoroughly ashamed of yourself.'

The older monk calmly replies, 'But I left her behind two hours ago. You are still carrying her.'

And with that, the elder monk continued to lead the walk, leaving the younger monk to contemplate his words for the remainder of the journey.

You don't need to be a Zen Buddhist to get the gist of that story.

We all go through times in life when other people say things or behave in a way that is hurtful towards us. Or simply when people do things differently from how we would do them.

How often do we carry around past hurts, holding on to resentments, jealousies and ill will when the only person we are really hurting is ourselves?

We can all too easily become attached to our resentments, stuck in them, to the point where we cannot see beyond blame and anger.

Blame and anger close us down. Compassion opens us up.

As we incline our hearts towards compassion, for ourselves and for others, we realize the opportunity to finally let go of resentment and blame. We are able to move away from narrow judgments on ourselves and others and realize a more open, expansive view, from which point we might be able to act more skilfully.

From this broader vantage point, we find that we do not have to be overwhelmed by hate and blame even though those feelings still arise. We might even find that forgiveness is possible even though we had long since decided that it was never on the cards.
And when those feelings do arise, as they surely will, maybe we can be mindful about them, understanding that

we have the option of acknowledging them and allowing them to pass rather than acting on them.

Each of us has the capacity to find forgiveness, patience and tolerance in our hearts.

Loving-kindness promotes wellbeing for all.
But it starts with you.
May you live with ease and with kindness.
May you respect yourself.
May you find healing.
May you rest in care and compassion.
May you abide in contentment and make room for joy in your life.
May you gladden the hearts of others and help them live in the deepest peace.

Home practice for week following session five

Three minute breathing space.

Listen to this guided meditation once a day on six days out of the next seven. Record any impressions on a sheet of paper each time you listen to the track.

Loving-kindness

There are three loving-kindness meditations available this week.
Listen to each of them twice for the next six days.
Use a notebook to record your experience.

NUTRITION - Week Five: Plants Do Matter for the Mind

This week's session emphasizes the importance of being kind to yourself. One of the kindest things we can do for our mind and body (apart from drinking enough water and eating slowly!) is to eat a diet high in plant foods. Plant foods provide the fibre and nutrients we require to improve our health on all levels. In fact, a good predictor of your continued good health and longevity is the diversity and the amount of plant foods you eat.

Fruits and vegetables contain tens of thousands of natural plant pigments with antioxidant, anti-inflammatory and anti-aging properties. Regular consumption of these health-promoting compounds protects us against chronic degenerative diseases, reduces inflammation and repairs DNA damage.

Sadly, these valuable plant compounds have considerably declined due to modern breeding methods and growing conditions. Wild apples, for instance, contain far more plant nutrients and less sugar than modern commercial eating apples!

Another reason to eat plant foods is for their fibre content. Vegetable and fruit fibre has a variety of important functions, and one of the most significant is encouraging the growth of 'friendly' flora in the digestive tract. Fibre is food for our microbes. We now understand that the more robust and diverse our gut flora, the greater the likelihood of maintaining good health, including brain health.

Researchers have found that people with a greater abundance of certain beneficial gut bacteria maintain better cognitive performance than those with a lower abundance. The diversity of your diet from plant foods drives a more diverse gut microflora.

Consuming the same (few) foods day in and day out simply won't encourage diversity.

If you are not already doing so, this week's message is an invitation to introduce as many colourful plant foods as you can (i.e. vegetables, fruit, herbs) into your daily diet. Ideally, 7 cups (equivalent to 7 fistfuls) of veggies plus 2 cups (fistfuls) of fruit – this is roughly 750g per day (pre-cooked).

Try to fit in as many different plant varieties each week (25-30 would be ideal according to Jeff Leach, founder of the Human Food Project). If this seems unimaginable, don't worry (!), it's much better for your digestion to start off slowly and increase the amount of plant foods you eat each day gradually but consistently. Your reward will be better digestion, clearer skin, better immunity, fewer hormonal issues, and most importantly, greater clarity and focus.

It's time to spoil yourself, and your bugs…mindfully.

Exercise:

The next time you go food shopping, spend a little time perusing the aisles in the produce department. Are there any fruit and vegetables you are unfamiliar with or haven't eaten for a while? Try out a new variety and eat local, seasonal and organically grown where and when you can.

Keep a tally of how many portions of fruit and vegetables per day you currently eat. Up your intake by one cup (fistful) daily each week. For example, if you eat 3 cups every day, then up your intake to 4 cups per day this week. Next week increase to 5/day…

"Eat food. Not too much. Mostly plants."
(Source: 'In Defense of Food: An Eater's Manifesto' by Michael Pollan, American author, journalist, activist, academic)

Jon's Reflections On Week Five

Reflections on loving-kindness meditations

When I was introduced to loving-kindness meditation, I slightly recoiled. For a short while, I thought that my worst fears about meditation were being confirmed.

It took me a few meditations but, slowly, I started to warm to it. This wasn't about casting lovey-lovey spells out into the universe. This wasn't about pretending that life is a bowl of cherries and that we should walk around grinning like Cheshire cats all day.

Until I started practicing loving-kindness I was completely oblivious to how much time and energy I devoted to holding on to grudges, even the most ancient of grudges. The family member I hadn't spoken to for so many years that I'd long forgotten what it was that we'd fallen out over. The work colleague who had once been flippantly dismissive about an article I'd written for a newspaper. The man in the park who'd called me 'an unfit dog owner' after Banjo had ambushed his family picnic and made off with a ham sandwich…

It was as though I had kept a mental card index of all the people who had ever slighted me. Whenever these people came to mind,

I was barely aware of the difficult thoughts and emotions that arose by way of response. I failed to see that this was an exhausting way to live and that it was avoidable.

Loving-kindness meditation helped me realise the sheer pointlessness of hanging on to grudges. A grudge only really impacts on me. More often than not, the person I feel grudgeful towards is completely oblivious to the fact that I'm continuing to be eaten up with blame and resentment. In effect, I'm prolonging my own suffering, needlessly.

I started to appreciate that, even if I was resistant to the idea of 'making it up' with those I had fallen out with, it was not necessary to hold on to old thoughts and old feelings about them.

Or, if those thoughts and feelings still persist, might it be possible to soften in relation to them?

Then there's self-compassion. Until I started loving-kindness meditations, I had no idea just how tough I was on

myself. I was certainly capable of being critical of others, but the harshest criticisms I reserved for myself. I didn't feel competitive with others but I was always in competition with myself, forever judging that I was coming up short. Had I compiled a life report to myself, it would have read, 'You could always do better.'

Within a few weeks of practice, I started to be kinder to myself. Instead of striving to match up to my own standards of what was acceptable, I began to accept that my best was good enough.

Feeling kinder towards myself, I found that being kinder to others came as a matter of course. Connecting with a sense of common humanity, I could see that everybody is suffering in this life, one way or another. We are all part of the human story and yet we go through our lives completely ignorant of the episodes that make up someone else's journey through life. But that doesn't stop us making flash judgments.

The bus driver isn't as polite as he might be when he hands me the ticket. 'He's rude. He shouldn't be in the job with manners like that…' Maybe he's simply having a bad day. A bad week. A life full of wretched luck. Maybe, if I pause for

just a moment, I can admit to myself that I know nothing about his story. In that mindful pause, maybe I can feel some compassion for him, quietly wish him ease of being and, in so doing, close the gap a little between myself and others.

The great thing about self-compassion and compassion for others is that it is never-ending. We can never exhaust it.

It is worth asking ourselves: How can I affect the quality of the day in a good way? Can I be kind? Can I be kinder?'

Can we stop thinking in terms of opponents and enemies? Can we look and find the good in people rather than the bad?

Can we let go of the heavy burden of blame?

Can we begin to cultivate a willingness to abide in kindness? Starting with a willingness to be kind to ourselves?

GERARD'S REFLECTIONS ON WEEK FIVE

Loving-kindness changed everything for me. Over the years, as I segued from youth to middle age, I lost something. I just wasn't sure what. Now, I think what I lost initially was the skill of being kind to myself, of being my own best friend.

Pressures of family and society to be a 'success' inevitably led to feelings of 'failure' whenever I failed to attain the standards set for me, and indeed by me.

I dealt with this by resolving to try twice as hard in future – doubling my standards and failing even harder. The vicious circle of too little compassion then inevitably led to a harder shell of self-defence and less compassion for others.

With loving kindness, for the first time in my life, I made a deliberate, conscious decision to fall in love with myself again - to forgive myself and to be kind to myself. The pressure that fell off my shoulders almost instantaneously was a revelation. As my shell softened, so too did my outlook on other people.

How did this occur? It started happening every time I forgave myself when distracted during a meditation. This in

turn developed into an absolute lack of judgment whenever thoughts turned up during meditation.

From there, the more often I meditated, the easier and more obvious it became to practice a loving lack of judgment toward myself and others in all kinds of life situations.

When people behaved in a way that I found really unpleasant*, I was able to ponder that if, up to that point, I had that person's DNA and life experiences, then I too would be behaving like that. This way I replaced anger or judgment or hostility with sympathy and an attempt to understand.

(* I choose my language very carefully in these situations – the words we use have a big influence on how we think. So judgmental concepts like 'bad' behaviour are particularly unhelpful for me.)

I started walking down the street repeating mantras to myself as I would in loving-kindness meditations at home, but simplified.

"May I be peaceful, may I be healthy, may I be happy". One of my favourites was to extend this to as many people as

practical as I walked down the street (silently of course). “May you be peaceful, may you be healthy, may you be happy”.

People ceased to be a mere backdrop to my walk and ‘came to life’. From the driver on the bus to the woman at the supermarket checkout, I started making a real point of not just thanking them, but really meaning it, making sure there was eye contact and sincerity. It felt good, as it continues to do. The giving of loving costs nothing and the more you give, the more you have left.

Previously, if I held a door open for someone (male or female) and they swanned through without saying thank you, I’d rage inside and at the very least would shout a loud, sarcastic ‚you’re welcome’ at them as they obliviously walked away. Silently sending them good wishes, I felt far better - I was taking back control of my reactions.

Love may not be all you need, but it's a wonderfully fulfilling and majorly rewarding part of what you need, for sure. So many people that come to BrightonMindfulnessCentre.com for courses come because they want to transform their lives. And so often, their lack of self-compassion is glaringly noticeable. The benefits

unfold as they rediscover something so often lost since childhood, if ever present previously.

A quote from an unlikely source stayed with me from my teenage years – Les Dawson, reflecting in his autobiography about the best advice he ever received:

Be kind.

FAQ FOR WEEK FIVE

With the loving-kindness meditations, I'm meeting some resistance, perhaps because I'm not exactly sure what my intention is meant to be. When I'm invited to wish ease of being on, say, a total stranger, or on every living creature, am I doing so in the hope that the other person(s) will somehow find some peace because I have sent this wish out into the universe? If so, it sounds a little optimistic. Thanks in advance.

Assuredly, you are not being invited to cast any spells here. Loving-kindness is really about cultivating a sense of self-compassion and compassion for others without seeking actual benefits. It's about connecting with what is truly in our hearts, discovering how wide our circle of compassion can reach.

Another way of putting it would be to say that, when we practice loving-kindness, we are planting seeds of kindness without worrying too much about the kind of harvest it will bring – without being too attached to outcome. Aside from the meditations, try it in your everyday life. See how being kinder to yourself and to others affects the quality of the day – not just your day, but that of everyone you come into contact with.

I've been following the course with no problems whatsoever but I've encountered my first real hurdle in week five's loving-kindness meditations. Wishing compassion and ease of being on myself, my friends, my family, I have no issue with that. But wishing compassion on everyone in the universe?! Including people I don't like?! That seems a bit 'out there' for me. How do I get over this hurdle?

It's important to remember that the loving-kindness meditations, like all the others on this course, are invitational. If you feel any resistance to any part of the guided meditations, be curious about that resistance. If you can, bring your awareness right up the edge of it, and notice your response. What exactly is being resisted here? Can you work with that resistance and even befriend it? That's part of the invitation.

You don't need to aim for the impossible here. Do as little or as much as you are comfortable with. You might even find that you are willing to tolerate a little discomfort along the way.

I've been enjoying the course and feel that I'm getting a lot out of it.

However, something odd has been happening this week. During sitting meditation I get a feeling of falling, then panicky, fearful thoughts arise. Why am I feeling this way?

Mindfully speaking, we would simply notice those sensations and fears - then return to the anchor (breath etc.). We're definitely not trying to ward them off or push them down. We are, in a very real sense, befriending them.

Try just noticing the sensations as they appear, and notice any thoughts and feelings (fear etc.) that arise before allowing them to pass. If the feelings persist, it might be advisable to consult your GP.

I keep hearing a lot about acceptance on this course and that's fine. But don't I need to understand something before I can begin to accept it? Otherwise, what am I actually accepting? Something I don't really understand? See what I mean? I guess I'm tying myself in knots about this.

Paradoxically, mindfulness seems to bed down deeper when little effort is made to understand it. Mindfulness is more caught than taught. It's a subtle wonder. Patience and self-compassion are the keys.
When you accept your experience fully, you are much less likely to get caught up in it, be defined by it, or feel overwhelmed by it. This is what we are practicing.

There are evolutionary, cultural, conditioning and habitual reasons why it is not particularly easy to remain attentive to experience in the present moment. Mindfulness teaches us how to undo our conditioning and our habits of mind by paying attention and opening up to our experience as it is, rather than what we think it is. When we are being mindful, we are meeting our own present moment experience with kindness and acceptance.

We learn how to be more mindful not by grasping a set of concepts, but by experiencing what it is like to meet all our experience whole-heartedly, without resistance.

SESSION SIX: BEFRIENDING THE DIFFICULT STUFF

'Doing more of what doesn't work, doesn't work.' (Nathaniel Branden)

'It is not life's events that are causing problems or stress. It is resistance to life's events that is causing this experience. Since the problem is caused by using your will to resist the reality of life passing through you, the solution is obvious - stop resisting.' (Michael Singer)

Theme For Session Six

In the pivotal sixth session of the course, we look at ways of gently turning towards difficulty.

For many people, this week of the course marks a decisive turning point.

We all come up against difficulty in our lives. Difficulty causes us pain and suffering, frustration and even helpless despair. So our natural response is to turn away from it in some way. If turning away solved the difficulty, all well and good.

But, of course, it rarely does.

As human beings, it seems perfectly natural that we tend to turn towards pleasant experiences and turn away from what

Shakespeare called 'the 'the slings and arrows of outrageous fortune.' But, when we turn away from unpleasant thoughts, feelings or body sensations, our problems seem to multiply. There is a quote attributed to Carl Jung, the world renowned Swiss psychiatrist and psychoanalyst, which has since been adopted by neuroscientists around the world.

'What we resist persists,' Jung apparently said, 'and what we resist not only persists. It grows in size.'

It is as though our minds and bodies are constantly sending out messages and signs. If we choose to ignore them, those messages and signs tend to get more and more insistent until they are noticed and accepted.

In the meantime, turning away from difficulties, we suffer. We are conditioned to want to fix things when they are not working to our satisfaction. This approach serves us well when a household appliance breaks down or when we break

a bone in our body. We fiddle about with the broken toaster until it is working again. We rush ourselves to A&E to get the broken arm seen to. When our feelings are unpleasant and difficult to be with, we have a tendency to believe that we can think our way out of them or simply wish them away. Experience tells us this approach doesn't work with emotions. They can't be fixed like a toaster or a broken limb.

As we've learned over the previous five weeks, mindfulness is really about opening to and staying with all present moment experience - pleasant, unpleasant and everything in between – directly, and with friendly curiosity. In this way we can transform the way we relate to ourselves, to others, and to the world of nature.

★

Turning point: In befriending difficulty, turning kindly towards it without judgment, rather than turning away from it, we facilitate both immediate and longer-term effects.

In the short term we begin to see how quick and keen we are to avoid dealing with the unpleasant in our lives. We become more attuned to the way negative thoughts give birth to anxious feelings which, in turn, give birth to disagreeable body sensations. And vice versa.

With practice, we can gently and skilfully undo the habitual reactions that seem to cause us so much suffering.
In the longer term, we develop more skillful ways of relating to troublesome experiences.

So many of us seem to be besieged by worry. In this way, human beings are noticeably different from other animals. Other animals might share similar traits to humans, including basic emotions and motivations, but they tend to react only to their immediate physical environment.

Humans react to their mental environment, the thoughts in their heads, as though they were real. The thoughts trigger body sensations and emotions. Yet, more often than not, the world we create with our thoughts bears scant resemblance to the world as it actually is.

We are possessed of highly sophisticated brains which enable us to look into the future, predict most likely scenarios, and plan accordingly.

These skills serve us well when making plans for next year's holiday so that we can secure the best prices for flights and hotels, take time off work and make sure that Auntie Joan is able to take care of the dog, the cat and the rabbit while we laze around on the Majorcan beach.

Our brains are also highly efficient problem-solving computers. If that long-anticipated holiday goes catastrophically wrong and you get robbed at gunpoint during your Majorcan sojourn, chances are that you will be enterprising enough to figure your way out of the tight spot you are in and make it home safe and sound.

The flipside of having such brilliantly sophisticated brains is that our highly active imaginations lend themselves to worry and wild speculation about what the future holds.

The Stone Age brains we still carry around with us make us hyper-alert to dangers and so we are prone to imagining worst-case scenarios, focussing on all the things that might

go wrong in the future, regardless of probability. Consequently, we find ourselves reacting to relatively small concerns as though they were life-threatening.

★

Turning point: Mindfulness teaches to see worries for what they are: speculative thoughts. By seeing them for what they are, we can avoid becoming entangled in them. Just as you are not your thoughts, you are not your worries.

Up until now on this mindfulness course, we have been practicing letting go of thoughts and moving our attention back to the focus of the meditation.

In week six we effectively do the opposite - leaning towards thoughts and feelings - particularly those we have some difficulty with, including our most persistent worries and emotional patterns - and being curious about them.

Staying with them for at least a few moments, we bring our curiosity to parts of the body where those thoughts and feelings are most obviously made manifest.

In the body scan we learned to breathe in and out of different body parts such as the small of the back and the shoulders. Now we do something very similar with 'difficult' sensations, gently softening towards them whilst reminding ourselves that they are ephemeral in nature and will doubtless pass.

So what happens if we simply turn towards them, gently acknowledge that they have arrived, accept them, allow them to be and allow them to dissipate.

That's what we are exploring in session six.

As ever, you are invited to conduct this exploration gently, and with self-compassion.

If parts of the various 'Turning Towards…' meditations prove to be too challenging, remember that you only need to stay with the intensity for as long as feels manageable for you in that particular moment.

The Guest House
By Rumi

This being human is a guest-house.
Every morning a new arrival.

A joy, a depression, a meanness,
some momentary awareness comes
as an unexpected visitor.

Welcome and entertain them all!
Even if they're a crowd of sorrows,
who violently sweep your house
empty of its furniture,

still, treat each guest honorably.
He may be clearing you out
for some new delight.

The dark thought, the shame, the malice,
meet them at the door laughing,
and invite them in.

Be grateful for whoever comes,
because each has been sent
as a guide from beyond.

Home practice for week following session six

Worry meditation

Listen to this guided meditation once a day on six days out of the next seven. Use a notebook to record your experience.

Turning towards difficulty

Listen to the shorter meditation (Turning Towards Difficulty (Shorter) for the first two days.

Listen to the Turning Towards Thoughts meditation on the next two days.

Listen to the Turning Towards Thoughts And Feelings on the following two days.

Three minute breathing space

Listen to this guided meditation once a day on six days out of the next seven. Use a notebook to record your experience.

NUTRITION - Week Six: Be Mindful of Sugar

For many people, food is a means to an end. Rarely do we actually have time or the presence of mind to stop and reflect what it is we are putting into our mouths and what its effects might be.

This is changing, as we become increasingly aware of just how much food affects our mental and physical health.

In a time-driven society, it's still a constant challenge not to succumb to processed convenience food and snacks such as crisps, sweetened drinks and chocolate.

This type of refined diet is high in sugar, salt, unhealthy type of fats, additives and low in fibre, vitamins, minerals and beneficial fats – all necessary ingredients, as we know, for lasting health and vitality. And a well-functioning brain.

Eating these pseudo-foods habitually may appear a matter of personal choice, as the manufacturers claim, yet they are carefully and scientifically constructed so as to bias our future food choices towards repeat purchases.

The notion that junk food possesses addictive qualities is gaining scientific credence - we may be more mindless than we care to admit!

My main pet 'hate', as far as convenience food goes, is the amount of sugar it contains. Most of us eat too much sugar because we love the taste, but the human body has not evolved to process chronic 'overdosing' of it very well.

Sugar, like other refined carbohydrates is "fast-releasing" - it provides a sudden burst in energy, followed by a slump and the desire for another sugar-fix.

The perpetual use of fast-releasing carbs upsets the hormonal status quo, leading to mood swings, poor concentration, weight gain, poor immunity and fatigue.

In the longer term, chronic blood sugar imbalance coupled with stress and a lack of exercise leads to degenerative diseases – including obesity, diabetes and heart disease and possibly dementia (Type 3 diabetes is a term that has been proposed for Alzheimer's).

We can't even escape the sugar trap by choosing unrefined sugar, honey, molasses, agave or maple syrup. These also provide concentrated forms of sweetness which have similar effects on the body. Artificial sweeteners aspartame, sucralose and saccharin should also be avoided.

Getting your blood sugar under control is the key to stable mood, better focus and concentration as well as losing weight and quite probably to a longer life!

BUT…. the natural workings of the body can override all reason and will-power. A quick-fix solution such as a chocolate bar, for example, keeps us going until the next energy crisis hits - and as we limp, rather like a clapped-out rollercoaster from one energy slump to the next, we are not surprisingly rather exhausted by the end of it all.

To wake up from a sugar-induced lethargic stupor, stay clear of overly refined and processed convenience foods. Slow-releasing foods, on the other hand, provide sustained energy (fresh fruit and vegetables, beans, pulses, nuts, seeds, wholegrains), so you are less likely to crave and binge.

'Slow-carbs' level out the road ahead, smoothing out the next highs and lows, and help you to kick the sugar habit for good. Also include small amounts of lean protein, essential fats and added nutrients to support glucose management. Exercise and the avoidance of stress and stimulants like caffeine and nicotine are important, too.

My advice is to scrutinise processed foods and not be bamboozled by wholesome images on the packaging. Check labels carefully to see whether the food actually contains the suggested nutritious items or is made mostly from artificial ingredients and fillers.

Be aware that words ending in "ose" (maltose, dextrose…) are actually sugars, and that low-fat or fat-free products usually contain high levels of sugar or sweeteners to compensate for lack of taste. You may even find it surprisingly difficult to 'mindfully eat' these factory concoctions once you ignore the pretty picture on the box – a sure signal to avoid them, or accept the health consequences!

Managing sugar cravings or issues with binge eating do respond well to nutritional therapy interventions, in particular where nutritional supplements compensate for a potential shortfall in dietary nutrients.

Exercise:

This week, be more mindful about how you feel, think and behave after consuming specific foods and drinks. Experiment with new snacks: you can try out some tasty examples here

http://thehealthbank.co.uk/top-ten-favourite-healthy-snacks/

'It is the awareness of the present moment, the realization of why we do what we do, that enables us to stop feeling bad and start changing our behavior.'

(from "Savor: Mindful Eating, Mindful Life"
by Thich Nhat Hanh and Lilian Cheung)

Jon's Reflections On Week Six

Reflections on the worry meditation

As far back as I can remember, I was always a big worrier. I got it from my mum. She used to say that she would even worry about her worries. I was much the same. Often, in the past, it felt like my mind was constantly seeking out things to worry about, problems to gnaw away at. It never seemed to stop.

My maternal grandmother was not a worrier and she was fond of telling me and my mother, 'Worry is like a rocking chair. It keeps you busy, but it never gets you anywhere.' That made perfect sense to me. But those wise words weren't much help to me at the time. At least, they didn't stop me from worrying.

During my teenage years, my energies either seemed to pour into the acutely painful self-consciousness of life in the moment or worries about the next moment, the next day, the next year, the rest of my life. Quicksands of disquiet on all sides. I was drawn to worst-case scenarios like a moth to a flame.

I guess I got to a point in my life where I was resigned to forever being a worrier. I'd tried everything including talking therapy and hypnosis. But nothing worked, at least not for long.
Mindfulness changed all that. I started to see that worries, however real they seemed to me, were only thoughts and it wasn't necessary to lose myself in their content.

What became obvious to me was that, somewhere along the line, I'd bought into the idea that worrying about stuff was somehow helping me to ward off the inevitable unpleasantness that life deals out. As though, if I was worrying about something, I was solving the problem that would lead to the unpleasantness.

Now I can see that all I was achieving by churning worries around in my head was causing myself a great deal of unnecessary anxiety and, meanwhile, setting myself further and further apart from what was actually happening in my life.

My wise old nan had another favourite saying about worry, which she claimed was of ancient Chinese origin. 'You might not have a choice when the birds of worry fly over

your head,' she would say, 'but you can prevent them building nests in your hair.'

When I was growing up, that saying didn't mean very much to me as, no matter how often I contemplated its innate wisdom, it didn't lessen my worries one little bit. Now, it makes complete sense to me. In fact, I've typed it out on a card and pinned it to the noticeboard in front of my desk. Every time I glance up and look at it, I think of my grandmother and I smile.

Reflections on turning towards difficulties

On my first ever mindfulness course, the 'turning towards' meditations marked a big turning point for me. A great deal of the suffering in my life (the anxiety, the depression, the almost constant sense of unease) had, I now realised, largely been caused by how I reacted to difficult thoughts and emotions.

When those difficulties arose, I would do just about anything to avoid them. I would try to run from them or distract myself from them. Anything but face them. For a long time in my adult life I used alcohol to numb the pain

that these difficulties brought. It had never occurred to me for a moment that turning towards difficulties would actually help alleviate them.

Like most people, I seemed to have a natural tendency to hold on to unpleasant experiences, to dwell on the negative, and to churn negative thoughts over and over to the point where I felt I might go mad.

All of this invariably came to a head for me during and after relationship break-ups. Even if I had been the one who'd decided that a relationship had run its course, I found it very difficult to emotionally unhook from that person and move on. Months would be spent ruminating on key moments in the relationship that had crashed…rehashing, remodelling…'What if…what if…what if…why?'

Though I'd never have admitted it to myself at the time, I had a pretty fixed idea about how a relationship should be: loving, romantic, without conflict. When conflict arose in a relationship, I would freeze, unsure of how to deal with it, and I would want to hide.

Looking back, I can see that what I was clinging to was the idea of a relationship that would deliver only pleasant experiences and none of the unpleasant stuff. In other words, I was attached to a fantasy of the perfect relationship in which there were never any disagreements, misunderstandings, awkward silences, slammed doors, disappointments or heartbreaking endings.

In some ways, it was as if I was embarking on the same relationship again and again and again, needing to heal ancient familial wounds, wanting people and situations to be a certain way rather than accepting and appreciating things just as they are.

Mindfulness gave me the space (the space around thoughts, the space around feelings, the space in my heart) to see all that clearly. Once it was seen, it could not be unseen.

Slowly, but surely, mindfulness has given me the confidence to turn towards difficulties and, degree by degree, lean in close to my fears, my worries, my self-doubts, right up to the strongest point of resistance.

In turning towards these difficulties rather than push them away or pretend they are not here, I have learned that there is nothing to fear. I've come to see that the suffering in my past largely arose from the resistance itself, and from the unnoticed habit of wanting things to be other than the way they really are.

To be in conflict with what is happening doesn't end suffering; the opposition to what is perpetuates the suffering. The way of personal transformation, the way to inner freedom, is to bring non-judging awareness to what is actually happening, to turn towards our experience with openness, acceptance and kind attention.

We start right here, exactly where we are, and not from where we would prefer to be. When we are centred in our own lives, when what is actually happening is not muddled by the mental overlay of worries, concepts and preconceptions, we might be able to see that there is nothing wrong with this moment. It simply is what it is. And it's nothing to be afraid of. As soon as we realise that, we can stop running away from our own lives. Just as I finally stopped running away from mine.

GERARD'S REFLECTIONS ON WEEK SIX

In all my brave (for me) words about loving-kindness at the end of the last chapter, one example stood out a mile for me and it involved turning towards the difficulty of my relationship with someone I knew.

I'd known this person a long time and for the past 10 years they seemed to have made a point of being unpleasant to, and about, me. It had been driving me mad, particularly as I didn't know what to do about it. This person delighted in crossing normally accepted lines of unpleasantness and using whatever they could to root out any Achilles heels and be as insulting as possible.

For years, I would get angry, hurt and frustrated. I would avoid any social situation where they would be present and spend hours dwelling on their cruelly devised put-downs.

I would turn away from this whenever I could, with the thought in my mind that I didn't want to become obsessed, but it always lurked there in my subconscious, always worse in the imagining that it could possibly be in the reality. Ignoring it only made it worse.

Loving-kindness clearly must hold the answer in situations like this, but how on earth could I break through the instincts of self-preservation and anger to achieve it?

This is where turning towards difficulty came in. It all started with noting how my body reacted when I had these feelings – the simple act of noticing my physical reactions immediately dissipated my focus on the past and future, catapulting me back into the present. To couple this with a non-judgmental curiosity opened up a whole new way of responding to this and other stressful situations.

Much of my anger was based in fear and this was the difficulty I finally turned towards once I knew how. Over time, I have come to accept that this person's behaviour is born of frustration and fear – a good tortured by its own hunger and thirst, as the saying goes.

I still don't go to social functions where the troublemaker is going to be, but now it's out of choice rather than a fear of what might happen. I feel only pity where once there was hatred. I hope for the best for them where I used to hope for the worst. It's all a lot easier and it takes a lot less energy.

Indeed, greater energy was another thing that came to the fore generally. I remember a moment when I was shown, to my amazement, how many programmes I was running in the background on my iPhone without even knowing. No wonder my batteries were running own so quickly.

The same with this course – it was the equivalent of shutting down all that stuff in the background so I could focus on one thing at a time. My focus became much better and my batteries didn't need so much charging.

Perhaps the biggest revolution in this segment of my life was knowing that I now had a toolkit for dealing with anything that might pop up in the future. I could walk through the present without that nagging fear in the back of my mind, much in the same way that Spiderman never has to be scared of being mugged. In turning towards difficulty, I robbed it of its power and discovered a deep peace and freedom that had been missing all my adult life.

FAQ FOR WEEK SIX

My practice is going OK. Depends on the day I guess. I do still run into self-criticism a fair bit though. It sometimes feels like self-hatred.

Any thoughts?

Regarding those self-critical thoughts or feelings of self-hatred, that's where the Turning Towards meditations can be particularly beneficial.

We learn to gently lean into thoughts and feelings that we've been conditioned to turn away.

We learn to lean into those thoughts and feelings rather in the way we perform a yoga stretch - going up to the limit of what we can deal with in that moment, and no more. Just as we learn not to overstretch in yoga, we learn to lean into thoughts and feelings as much as we're able to.

Self-compassion is vital in this part of the practice. It's also important to be aware of our limits.

I mainly came to mindfulness because I'm a terrible worrier. I seem to be worrying less now, largely thanks to mindfulness practice. But I worry about distancing myself from life with mindfulness. Is that a possibility?

Regarding worries, we are all naturally choosy about the thoughts we have. We love warm, positive thoughts and we'd rather not have any prickly, worried thoughts at all. Mindfulness doesn't discriminate. It's not teaching us to live so that we only have positive thoughts and banish our worries.

We learn to appreciate all thoughts as thoughts and to see them for what they are – passing mental events. Some thoughts we can choose to act on; others we allow to pass, without getting caught up in their content.

Mindfulness is not about distancing yourself from life. Quite the opposite. It is about forging a more intimate connection with yourself, with others and with the natural world. What we are distancing ourselves from, if anything, are the needless dramas that we overlay on experience.

Mindfulness teaches us to drop the narratives that turn our everyday experiences into problems.
In doing that, we are better able to align with our direct experience from moment to moment.

Often it is the worrying that is the true cause of distancing yourself from life (which, remember, is only ever lived in the present). For some, it is tempting to look at worrying as some kind of safety net that will remind you not to put your hand in the fire. But the reality is that you're usually vastly overcompensating and needlessly running your battery down.

One thing I have noticed is that I occasionally feel detached from my body during sitting meditation and body scans. It's quite a nice feeling but I worry that it means I'm not meditating properly.

Any comments would be appreciated.

That sounds like an interesting experience but mindfulness isn't really about disidentifying from body or mind. Remind yourself that mindfulness practice is more about gently

zoning in than zoning out. It's about participating whole-heartedly with life's natural flow.

When we are being attentive to our experience in the moment, we adopt a wider perspective on our thoughts, feelings and body sensations – the totality of our experience. But this does not entail a distancing or a disconnecting. It actually entails a closing of the gap between ourselves and whatever is arising in the present moment.

I've been sailing through this course. Really loving it. But I've hit a bit of a brick wall with 'turning towards difficulty'. It's bringing up stuff, emotional stuff, that maybe I don't want to face right now.

What happens if I don't feel ready to turn towards certain difficulties at certain times?

Sometimes the 'turning towards difficulty' stage of the 8-week course is read as a demand rather than what it really is: an invitation. The time is not always right to turn towards difficulty.

One can acknowledge that the difficulty is there and then return to it another time. And do bear in mind that you are not required to jump straight in at the deep end. Think of it as a learning curve. Start with difficulties on the less challenging end of the scale and only move on to more emotionally loaded stuff when you feel good and ready.

I've been reading a fair bit about meditation (various kinds). It sounds like some people have big breakthroughs. It makes me wonder why I haven't had one! I do feel more aware these days. But I wonder if I've made a big enough 'jump'. Any advice?

Everybody experiences meditation differently and at their own pace. Don't be concerned about big breakthroughs. At this early stage, the fact that you feel more aware is something to cherish. Again, it's worth reminding yourself not to be goal-orientated and not to judge yourself. Meditate to meditate. The rest will surely follow.

SESSION SEVEN: RESTING IN AWARENESS

'Is the beam from a lighthouse affected by howling wind and rain? It remains perfectly steadfast and unaffected by the storm. Your true self is like that. Nothing can ever harm you once you are consciously aware that it is so.' (Vernon Howard)

'Show up. Pay attention. Tell your truth. Be open to outcome.' (Angeles Arien)

Theme For Session Seven

In the seventh session of the course, we take stock of how far we've come and explore the themes of wholeness and spaciousness.

Firstly, let us reflect a little on the formal meditations we have been working with these past six weeks.

* In the raisin exercise, you were invited to approach the raisin almost as if you were a visitor from a distant planet encountering this piece of fruit for the very first time, paying attention with each of your senses in turn.

In bringing bare attention to a raisin, a foodstuff we normally devour without giving it much, if any, attention, we are reminded just how often we eat with almost complete lack of awareness. Often, we are barely aware of the smell, taste and texture of the food we are shovelling into our bodies at each mealtime.

* In the body scan you anchored your awareness by bringing moment to moment attention to sensations in key body parts, registering when your mind had wandered.

* With mindful movement, we took a different look at how the body can ground us in the moment. Through a series of small, seemingly inconsequential movements, we explored how bringing curiosity to bodily reactions can open up new ways of relating to ourselves.

Like the body scan, mindful movement teaches us to listen more closely to what our bodies are telling us.

* In the breath and body meditation, you continued to focus on noticing, acknowledging and bringing your attention back when your mind wandered.

In this meditation, both breath and body serve to anchor you firmly in the present moment.

Each time we bring awareness to our breathing, whatever we are doing, we will immediately be more present with our experience. As we tune in to our present moment experience, we are able to adopt a far more skilful and flexible relationship to what we find challenging or unpleasant.

We do this simply by dropping our attachment to the idea that this moment should be different from what it is and simply opening up to our present moment experience with kindness and curiosity.

* With the three-minute breathing space you were introduced to a kind of mini-meditation. It is important to reiterate that the breathing space ought not to be regarded as an alternative to the longer sitting meditations you are now familiar with. Instead, it is to be regarded as an important meditation in its own right. Offering a spacious, non-judgmental way to reconnect with the present moment and to your immediate experience, the breathing

space is easily adaptable to suit any situation you find yourself in. Also it can be any length you choose.
It is especially useful when life is at its most fraught and demanding.

The breathing space provides a convenient bridge between the formal practice of meditation which we will usually do on our own with time set aside for it, and the informal practice of mindfulness in our everyday lives.

In time, with practice, we will be able to introduce the breathing space more spontaneously, at times when we are feeling stressed or experiencing something unpleasant. In these situations, we are not using the breathing space to block or to get rid of these difficult experiences. Instead, we will be learning to bring more awareness to our reactions and to notice how we might resist what is occurring at these times.

* With the breathing/body/sound/thought meditation, we are invited to hear the sounds around us purely as sounds, noticing our tendency to judge them (as good, bad or indifferent) and observing how they arise and fall away.

Also we looked at how our engagement with thoughts can lead to suffering. Rather than see thoughts purely as passing mental events, a process of movement, we regard them as facts and get drawn into their content. We become so attached to our thinking that we allow thoughts to define who we actually are. The stories we tell ourselves become real. When thoughts become eternal truths, when we allow our thoughts to create our reality, they can easily overwhelm us and even shape our entire sense of self. Thus we become slaves to our thinking rather than using thinking as a tool.

As the old saying goes: the mind is a great servant but a terrible master.

And so we become preoccupied with thoughts about the past, immersed in thoughts about the future and, as we provide a running commentary on what is happening right now, we also become lost in thoughts about the present.
With practice, mindfulness can undo these mental tendencies so that the mind becomes less reactive.
Remember. We are not attempting to stop our thoughts. Instead, we learn that it is possible simply to allow thoughts to arise by themselves and to fade away accordingly. We

learn that we can choose which thoughts to act on and those we opt not to follow.

* Through loving-kindness meditation, we explored ways of cultivating both self-compassion and compassion for others, learning that long-held habits of reactive anger and blame can be undone if we can only bring ourselves to hold the moment in gentle awareness.

Making a habit out of paying attention to our present moment experience and cultivating the intention to be more compassionate, we start to notice which habits cause suffering to ourselves and others.

* With the Turning Towards…meditations, we looked at ways of gently turning towards thoughts, feelings and body sensations. However counter-intuitive it might sound, leaning towards these experiences can make them much easier to live with. We learn that much of our suffering is caused by our reactions to a situation rather than the situation itself.

Though mindfulness as we teach it on the Turning Point and Ninth Week courses is purely secular, it is occasionally

useful to mention ideas that have their roots in Buddhism. For example, Buddhist teachings pronounce that, when we suffer misfortune, two arrows fly our way. The first arrow is the actual unpleasant event, which can actually cause pain. The second arrow represents our reaction to the bad event. You don't need to be a Buddhist to recognise that experience. Indeed, if you notice your reactions to misfortunes in the light of this you'll often find that the second arrow is causing a large percentage of the discomfort.

Turning point: Often, pain cannot be avoided. A certain amount of pain in life is inevitable and unavoidable. But suffering is just one of many possible responses to pain. Suffering, in that sense, is optional as we have a choice as to how we respond.

Let us look at one example of how this can work.

First there is the difficulty. Let's say that you wake up with a pain in the small of the back.

There's the actual pain. Then there's your reaction to the pain.
You don't like it. You want it to go away. You tell yourself it is not fair that you are feeling this way. You tell yourself that it will spoil your day. You tell yourself that that this pain is unlikely to go away and will probably spoil your entire life...

In the meantime, you might take pause and decide that the wisest and most mindful course of action might be to call an osteopath and arrange a consultation.

The invitation is to bring awareness to the way we react to difficult experience. We can notice the non-acceptance and aversion in our experience: the resisting, tensing, bracing, numbing, the pushing away, the strong urge to distract ourselves from whatever is occurring…

We might notice how none of this makes the problem go away.

Indeed, it often intensifies our suffering.

★

Turning point: With practice we can mindfully accept what is already there, soften towards it and hold it in awareness. If we are not resisting it, objecting to it, perhaps it is no longer objectionable. It is no longer a problem. It just is. Then we can simply notice, without holding; allowing to be; allowing to pass.

Acceptance, in this sense, does not mean that we have to like what we are experiencing. Nor, in terms of mindfulness, does acceptance equate with passive resignation. We can recognize that, within spacious awareness, we actually have a choice.

We might choose to take decisive action. In some situations the wisest course of action might be to do nothing - or simply wait.

From one perspective, mindfulness is all about space or, more specifically, it is about realising the space around things. The space around thoughts. The space around feelings. The space around situations. Within that space, we

see more clearly the options that present themselves. A wider sense of perspective emerges.

In that space we find the room that's needed for whatever is going on in our lives at that moment. How many times in our lives do we find ourselves saying, 'I can't cope' or 'This misery will never end'. But we do cope and our situation changes. This is worth remembering: all things must pass.

No longer at the mercy of our own reactions, we can appreciate that it is possible find a natural space in the moment, a space which allows us to respond calmly and wisely. This marks a radical shift in how we relate to our own experience.

This space opens up to us naturally as we sharpen our attentional skills.

This idea is beautifully illustrated by a quote from Viktor Frankl, an Austrian psychiatrist who courageously endured imprisonment in Nazi concentration camps (he survived four camps, including Auschwitz) during World War II. In his extraordinary memoir, Man's Search For Meaning,

published in 1946, Frankl describes how he found meaning in spite of - and because of - the suffering all around him.

Frankl wrote, 'Between stimulus and response there is a space, and in that space lies our power and our freedom.'

Essentially, Frankl is saying that, while he had no choice at all about how he was treated in the camps and he had no choice about how those around him were treated, he realised that he did have a choice in how he responded to circumstances, from moment to moment.

Psychologist/author Elisha Goldstein elaborates on this point: 'In essence, the practice is to notice when the judging is happening so we can recognise the space in between what we're judging (the stimulus) and the judging itself (the reaction) and choose to make a change. The power to choose our responses comes with an awareness of that space.'

Recognising that this space is always available to us, we are able to move towards a sense of wholeness, towards a way of living where we are not at the mercy of our reactive, destructive cycles.

Because you feel angry, it does not mean that you need to behave aggressively. In a mindful space, the anger can be noticed and allowed to pass. In that mindful space, we are able to find perspective in the midst of strong emotions and the maelstrom of negative thoughts.

By shifting attention from the emotion and the thought to noticing the emotion and thought without becoming consumed by them, an entirely different experience presents itself.

'I go among trees and sit still.
All my stirring becomes quiet
Around me like circles on water.
My tasks lie in their places
Where I left them, asleep like cattle.'
(Wendell Berry)

When we respond to the moment mindfully, we are able to live more in the flow of life. We start feeling more free, more peaceful, less fragmented, less alienated.

Living more with a sense of wholeness it's likely that, whatever our burden in life - anxiety, depression, addiction, disability, phobia - we will be better equipped to relate to

our situation, better able to live in the moment as fully and as wisely as we can.

We might find ourselves thinking, 'this all sounds well and good but it's never going to happen to me. That kind of freedom is for others. It's not something that I'm ever going to experience.'

But Viktor Frankl showed that this kind of freedom is within touching distance for us all, whatever our circumstances. Even in the midst of the most appalling suffering imaginable, Frankl was able to show that, if we hold our present moment experience in awareness, we can choose our response to circumstances, any circumstances. No exceptions. The whole of life is up for grabs here.

For Frankl, that discovery gave him the will to live through the Holocaust. Bearing the seemingly unbearable, realising that he was able to skilfully respond to life rather than live as though he had no choices, Frankl found his life's meaning.

Another famous Frankl quote is, 'Every human being has the freedom to change at any instant.'

Turning point: Being attentive to the fact that you have come up against an obstacle is the first step to overcoming it. The sooner you recognise it as an obstacle, the easier it will be to get past it.

You will find that many meditators, even long-term practitioners, come up against the very same impediment. More often than not, the apparent block is a mental one. A thought ('I really can't be bothered to meditate today – I've got a million other things to be getting along with'). Just like any other thought. Not a fact. Just a passing mental event.

Besides, meeting obstacles is a great opportunity to stretch ourselves and teach ourselves learn new skills.

This is well worth remembering on your mindfulness adventure. Maybe you will have days when your practice feels like tough going, when you wonder whether you are resilient or disciplined enough to keep going.

If you encounter an obstacle in your mindfulness practice, (some kind of resistance to sitting, perhaps), it might be tempting to think that you have failed in some way or that you have simply come up against an obstacle you can't get past.

But life will always present obstacles.

Remember that you can begin again at any moment and that we can only ever start from where we are in this moment, not from where we should be or from where we would like to be. You can begin again with the very next breath.

The turning point, if you haven't already reached it, is only ever a moment away. A mere breath away.

In this seventh week, we introduce you to three new meditations.

The lake meditation and the mountain meditation invite you to loosen your attachment to a fixed idea of self and allow yourself to 'become' the majesty, the hugeness and the stillness of nature.

You are invited to notice how the lake and the mountain remain grounded in what they are despite the constant whirl of changefulness happening all around.

With conscious awareness, it might be possible to glimpse the truth that our mental picture of ourselves is merely a composite of thoughts, fantasies and plans. It is the idea of ourselves as a solid, fixed self, rather than an ever-changing matrix of sensory impressions, that makes us experience ourselves as separate and alone. Einstein described this idea of a fixed self as 'an optical illusion of consciousness'.

Sometimes we feel separate from experiences, sometimes fully connected. Mindfulness helps us to become more in tune with these experiential shifts and helps us come to a clearer understanding about the role of 'self' in our everyday experiences. We might come to see that, while we require a separate sense of ego or self to function in the world, there is no solid, independent entity that existed in the past, exists now, and will exist in the future. What actually exists, perhaps, is something more akin to an experiential process subject to constant change.

When we cling to the idea of a fixed self, a kind of unchangeable inner controller, it follows that we become attached to a particular fixed representation of ourselves. We tell ourselves, 'I am a shy person', 'I am an anxious person' or 'I am the kind of person who is incapable of change.' Until we pay attention, it might not occur to us that these are only vague beliefs, bundles of unexamined thoughts.

Mindfulness helps us gain an experiential focus and, in so doing, we can begin to view the self from a far broader perspective. When we see that there is no self that is always the same, there is less focus on the narratives spun by our minds, the stories we tell ourselves about ourselves. When we cease believing that we are, as Alan Watts put it, 'isolated egos inside bags of skin', our lives feel less contracted, less isolated.

With practice, we can begin to let go of our inclination to divide up the world and relinquish the idea that we are separate from all other things. We can begin opening to the sense that, ultimately, everything is connected and everything simultaneously affects everything else – an idea fully supported by quantum physics.

If we can see through the notion of a fixed self at the centre of a universe, we can stop taking life so personally and choose not to get so caught up in daily dramas.

Holding our moment to moment experience in awareness, we can allow thoughts and feelings to come and go, without getting stuck in their content.

In the choiceless awareness meditation, we are invited to let go of the idea of directing attention to one particular anchor such as breath, body or sound. Instead, attention becomes more open and expansive, effectively going wherever it is drawn.

Meanwhile, we maintain our awareness in the present moment. We are invited to simply attend to whatever arises in the sphere of our experience as it arises and passes away, comes and goes, appears and disappears - without holding to anything.
If we get lost, we simply return to a familiar object of awareness, such as the breath, to bring us back to the present moment.

Home practice for week following session seven

Listen to the Mountain Meditation, the Lake Meditation and the Choiceless Awareness Meditation twice during the week.

NUTRITION - Week Seven: Building the Foundations for Your Mind

This week, we continue our exploration into practical nutritional strategies to support positive mental health, and expand the potential of our newfound mindfulness. We'll look at some of the basic requirements for the structure and function of our brains.

Just consider this: in the UK, in recent years we have seen a huge increase in anti-social behaviour, mood and neurological disorders, and learning difficulties.

No attention is paid to the essential role of diet in the official assessment or management of these conditions, yet many well-regarded studies (including those on prison populations) have clearly shown how diet and behaviour are intimately connected. For our brains to work effectively, the brain needs effective nutrients…

Nutritionists are particularly concerned about people consuming the "right" type of fats, because it has long been established that essential fatty acids (EFAs), obtained from food, are vital for brain development. Did you know that 60% of your brain consists of fats?

EFAs are components of our cell membranes, affecting the flexibility and permeability of all body cells. They prevent loss of moisture from our skin and mucous membranes and are mediators in controlling blood pressure, immunity and many other physiological activities. The body cannot manufacture its own precious EFAs, so we are entirely dependent on dietary sources.

For optimal brain health, we need to obtain enough of two groups of EFAs: omega-6 and omega-3 in the right proportions. The omega-6's are found in nuts, seeds and vegetable oils.

Avoid the highly inflammatory processed supermarket vegetable oils, though, and choose instead extra-virgin, cold-pressed organic olive and coconut oils. Avocados are good, too! Forget about margarine, and choose grass-fed butter as a spread.

The richest source of the anti-inflammatory omega-3's comes from cold-water fish, and there are smaller amounts in flaxseed, chia seeds and walnuts.

There is, however, considerable individual variation in our ability to convert the simpler essential fats from plants into the required forms of omega-3s (found already 'ready-made' in fish and seafood), called EPA and DHA.

Furthermore, some people have higher dietary requirements for omega-3s than others. The omega-3 fats, EPA and DHA, are absolutely critical for the structure and function of the brain - they provide its key building blocks.

Experts recommend that we should be eating two to four portions of fish per week, particularly oily fish such as wild salmon, sardines, pilchards, herring, trout or mackerel.

Although some types of fish may carry contaminants, the benefits from consuming seafood (preferably from sustainably managed sources) are likely to outweigh any risks.

In addition to the beneficial fats, we also require amino acids from protein foods for normal brain chemistry. Amino acids make neurotransmitters including serotonin and dopamine - important brain chemicals that affect mood, sleep, behaviour, attention and motivation.

A very restrictive diet or an inability to digest protein well may cause an imbalance in brain biochemistry. We are all unique in our protein needs: our age, gender, weight, health and activity levels determine how much protein we require and this can vary from day to day.

Here's a good rule of thumb: replace a high carb diet consisting of packaged and processed foods with 3 servings/ day of fresh meat, fish, chicken or eggs and whole grains, fruits and vegetables. If you are vegan, you can obtain protein from a variety of plant foods, including lentils, beans, soy foods, whole grains, nuts, seeds, and even vegetables.

Protein powders/shakes can be valuable additions - feel free to email me for advice on superior products, rather than those filled with sugar, artificial sweeteners, preservatives and other dodgy ingredients.

Ensure your digestion is working well and that you don't feel 'stuffed' and bloated or suffer with indigestion after eating. This may indicate low stomach acid and adversely affect protein digestion. It can be easily remedied – please contact me at martina@thehealthbank.co.uk rather than suffer in silence.

Finally, although a one-size-fits-all approach for a happy brain does not exist, ensure it is 'fit for purpose' with a good daily dose of essential fatty acids and amino acids!

Exercise

This week, make a written menu plan before doing your weekly shop, and include 2-4 portions of fish (or plant food alternatives if vegan/vegetarian). In addition, become more mindful of your daily protein intake.

If you would like some help with planning, check out my free e-book "Healthy Eating on a Budget". It includes a menu, recipes and shopping list at http://thehealthbank.co.uk/healthy-eating-on-a-budget-2016/

Jon's Reflections On Week Seven

Reflections on the mountain and lake meditations

When I look back on my life, it seems obvious to me that I was present for very little of it. This particularly hits home when I recall the times I have spent in beautiful locations.

During my time as a journalist, I found myself being flown regularly to impossibly exotic and exciting places to interview famous rock stars/actors/sportspeople and to cover movie shoots.

This was my job and I was grateful for the fact that it rarely felt like a job at all. Even so, I was rarely happy on those trips.

One scenario in particular sticks in my memory. In 1998, GQ magazine dispatched me to Los Angeles to interview the movie actor Mickey Rourke. At the time, Rourke was attempting some kind of comeback after years of personal and professional setbacks. I was scheduled to stay in LA for two nights but ended up staying for ten days. For reasons never explained, Rourke kept cancelling our interview and so my return was delayed, then delayed some more.

On the face of it, life could not have been sweeter. I was staying at one of LA's most exclusive hotels, a minute's walk from Santa Monica beach, all expenses paid. And I was there to interview one of my favourite actors, the star of movies like Rumblefish and Diner.

And yet, all I remember about that trip was the feeling of deep dread which consumed me from the moment I landed in California to the moment I departed. Crawling from the wreckage of a ten-year marriage at the time, it seemed like every moment was unbearably painful.

Wherever I went, whatever I did, the pain was there, unavoidable, inevitable, unyielding. Even when I finally got to visit Rourke at his Hollywood Hills villa, there was no respite. If anything, he was in a worse state than me. 'You can't imagine what it's like to live in my head,' he told me that afternoon. 'I wouldn't wish it on my worst enemy. It's as far from happiness as you can possibly imagine.'

Looking back on that trip and the months of driveling misery that followed it, I realize I had no chance because I didn't have the first clue about how to cope with the continual waves of sadness and despair that overwhelmed

me. Or the fearful, anxious, fiercely critical thoughts that besieged me, day and night: dark ruminations about the past, dark premonitions about the future – all these thoughts congealing into delusory outgrowths of apparent truth.

Apart from the fact that I felt awful throughout that entire trip, I remember very little else about those ten days by the beach in California. I can only suppose that I spent most of the time holed up in my hotel room, feeling close to despair, too afraid to move in case it made me feel ever worse.

I doubt it occurred to me even for a moment to take a walk on the soft sand beach, sit and watch the tide come in, maybe spot a few of the endangered snowy plovers that are known to nest in the area.

Sometimes I wonder how much difference it would have made if I knew then what I know now. A huge amount, I suspect. All the difference in the world. What I didn't know then was that I didn't have to believe all the thoughts that were swarming around my head – the ones that told me that I would never get over my broken marriage, that I'd always feel this desperately alone, that I'd never find another partner who would make me happy, that I'd never ever feel comfortable in my own skin.

I didn't know then that trying to push away unpleasant feelings or attempting to think my way out of them would never work. I had yet to learn that, in turning towards unpleasant experiences, there is a chance we may be able to be intimate with them, to be more at ease with them, to accept them.

When we shine the light of attention on them, it is often the case that they will lose their power over us. We can learn to be with our difficult thoughts, feelings and body sensations, without being lost in them.

When I think of that 37-year-old version of myself sitting in that Los Angeles hotel room, deep in the slough of respond, I feel enormous compassion for him. He sometimes crosses my mind when I sit and practice the lake or mountain meditations.

Feeling at peace, connected to the universe, dwelling in an infinite space of awareness, I bring him to mind and wish that he too had known how to be at home in the present moment. Then I realise, with an abrupt shock, that I'm at home right now, quietly resting in aliveness.

Reflections on the choiceless awareness meditation

I warmed to the choiceless awareness meditation almost immediately, loving the sense of freedom it offered, the simplicity of it – the invitation to pay attention to whatever arises in the moment, rather than directing myself in a precise way, using specific anchors (breath, body parts, sound etc.)

It quickly became my preferred meditation and one that I found easy to fold into my everyday life.

If I was showering, my attention might alight on the feeling of water on my skin. Out walking, I could notice my wandering thoughts and return to the moment by being attentive to the colour of the sky, the sound of traffic or children playing, the sensation of walking, the smell of freshly-baked bread wafting from a bakery doorway, the aftertaste of a good cup of coffee…all of it gently held in an open awareness.

Knowing that I could use everything, absolutely everything, to ground me in the moment helped me steady my internal

anchor at times when the waves got choppy – when life presented me with experiences that generated anxious thoughts and feelings. In that open awareness, troublesome thoughts and emotions would lose their momentum and I was better able to experience reality as it is, and hold it lightly. It enabled me to be more flexible and more adaptive in my responses to situations.

With open, choiceless awareness as my intention, I found that I was far less likely to drift unconsciously into old habits, like flotsam swept on the water. Immersing myself in the completeness of the moment gradually became my standard setting.

GERARD'S REFLECTIONS ON WEEK SEVEN

Resting in awareness. That's what meditation is for me – taking a well-earned rest. I look forward to it as I would look forward to a night at the cinema or theatre. I know I'll feel better afterwards and I also know that, on the days when it feels really difficult, those are the days I need it most and I'm getting most out of it.

This chapter talks about pain. I live in a small flat and walk around barefoot on the carpet most of the time. Consequently I stub my toe quite often. This used to be a high-drama moment with lots of jumping around and the choicest of swear words as I allowed all my emotions to be cranked up to 11.

Then I read something about most pain being nothing more than acute pressure and many things fell into place: 90% of my pain wasn't the physical sensation at all, but the narrative I was building around it.

‘Why didn't I see the chair leg before I stubbed my toe on it? I'm such an idiot! I could have avoided that. I can't believe I've done it again. This pain is extreme. I hate it and I want it to go away.’

And so on. Once I'd entertained the concept that 'you are not your thoughts', I realised I could change the narrative of harsh self-criticism and needless melodrama.

Over time, the triggers disappeared. Instead, I could be curious about this 'extreme pressure', which was really not much more than a rapid throbbing in my toe. The pain didn't

disappear, but it was reduced to maybe 10% of what it was previously, which was astonishing.

Addiction & Bad Habits

I came to mindfulness meditation with an unhealthy collection of bad habits that I'd developed to cope with the trauma and difficulties I'd gone through in life. The biggest of these was self-medicating with alcohol, a habit that had contributed to the early onset of diabetes and caused a thousand other problems in my life.

As the self-medicator so often does, I shored up all my justifications and banished any painful self-judgments by developing a cosmetically thicker skin. I lived in acute fear of anyone pointing out the truth and reacted aggressively (inside) if anybody strayed near that truth.

Resting in awareness and knowing that awareness was based in self-love and compassion, finally gave me the space to look at these issues straight on - where loving-kindness meets turning towards difficulty, the potential for radical transformation can be realised.

No longer was there a knee-jerk narrative of potential fear and pain to lock me into unhelpful ways of behaving. Now I had a choice. Not between right or wrong, good or bad... just a choice: more options.

I'm aware that many people will come to this book carrying unhelpful habits and addictions of their own. If you're one of those, here's a quick resume of how I used mindfulness and resting in awareness to transform that part of my life:

1. Stepping back from the situation and looking at it not with judgment, but compassion. Recognising what's going on and what's causing the triggers to the bad behaviour.

2. Accepting it, because it already is. Killing off any thoughts of self-judgment. At first, I was simply observing my behaviour, not trying to change it overnight. This was a radical change for me in the way I looked at things away from the yo-yo-ing of attempted self-denial and towards lasting change.

3. Becoming curious. Knowing there was no longer any judgment, I had the courage to look in detail at the processes that led me to the off-licence and once back home, led the drink to my lips. Knowing 'you are not your

thoughts' let me look at the cause and effect triggers - the habitual lies I told myself - that were going on in my mind. All without judgment, all without effort.

4. Noting body sensations when turning towards the difficulty. Paying attention to the moment instead of projecting into the next moment or the last. Simply making a note of how everything felt. When brought into awareness, out of the shadows of unconsciousness, these feelings inevitably dissipate.

This is necessarily a short and basic summation of things; a whole one would take a book (so watch this space). But, over a period of months after this course, my drinking subsided of its own volition. It didn't stop completely, but it came down to levels largely accepted as healthy.

I simply gave myself more choices - an extra gear in the car of my mind, rather than determinedly chugging away in second gear for the rest of my life. As this chapter says, and it's worth repeating:

"Recognising that this space is always available to us, we are able to move towards a sense of wholeness, towards a way of living where we are not at the mercy of our reactive, destructive cycles."

This is not a fairy story where I end up in the Garden of Eden without any problems and live happily ever after. It would be dishonest to present it like that - life isn't like that. But nonetheless, life has changed completely. I may get dealt the same cards, but I know how to play them very differently now.

FAQ FOR WEEK SEVEN

I wonder if it is possible to balance my hopes, dreams, and desires with the inevitable shadow that follows such ambitions - i.e. the fear of not realising them. Or is the concept of achieving goals and performing at one's best a contradiction in terms in the context of mindfulness? Should I simply strive to be my best in the moment, and place little hope and ambition towards the future?

It's more about being present with an open heart to whatever is arising in this moment.

Mindfulness tends to bring an all-round sense of being more at ease with oneself and the world. Consequently, plans are made from a more relaxed, more considered place.

The prize is realising that just about everything is OK in the moment if we're not agonising about it.

Self-compassion and non-judgment are key to this.

You are not being asked to give up hopes and dreams, assuredly. Though it pays not to become too attached to their outcomes.

I am now in the seventh week of the course. Some days are good with meditation, some days are difficult. Generally, I feel calmer now but I don’t think I am much happier. I guess I just keep trying, right?

Inevitably, meditation will offer up a mixed bag of experiences.

However regularly we practice, our lives will veer into choppy waters from time to time and we will be caught unawares.

But mindfulness is all about facing what comes up in our lives - good and bad, pleasant and unpleasant. It will never take us to a place where we’re able to handle everything easily. To expect that would be striving towards some kind of perfection and would therefore be counter-productive.

Keep practicing. That's probably a better way of thinking about it than trying to be happy. Also remember that, rather like trying to watch the hands of a clock move, positive change isn't always visible at every stage of the journey.

?

After seven weeks of practice, I still seem to be very caught up in outcomes. I can't seem to unhook from how things should turn out and I get disappointed when things don't turn out as I hoped - especially dates with women!
Any advice?

Maybe this little story will help…

There was an old farmer who had worked his crops for many years. One day his horse ran away. Upon hearing the news, his neighbours came to visit. "Such bad luck," they said sympathetically. "Maybe," the farmer replied.

The next morning the horse returned, bringing with it three other wild horses. "How wonderful," the neighbours exclaimed. "Maybe," replied the old man. The following day, his son tried to ride one of the untamed horses, was thrown, and broke his leg.

The neighbours again came to offer their sympathy on his misfortune. "Maybe," answered the farmer. The day after, military officials came to the village to draft young men into the army. Seeing that the son's leg was broken, they passed him by.

The neighbours congratulated the farmer on how well things had turned out. "Maybe," said the farmer.

Food for thought?

It is human nature to imagine how certain scenarios will play out but they rarely unfold exactly as we wish them to. Even then, getting what we think we want can sometimes be a mixed blessing, as the above story implies.

On dates, try to let go of specific expectations about how the evening will play out. Accept that you cannot predict how the date will go. Be open to whatever arises and whatever occurs.
Practically speaking, bring what you have learned on the course to the date – before, during and after.

Before: Being mindful about anxious thoughts in the lead-up to the date. Focus on the journey rather than the destination – this could literally be the journey to the meet-up, no reason not to enjoy that - or perhaps more usefully, a

focus on enjoying the evening for its own sake rather than getting caught up in worries or expectations about where it might lead.

During: Bringing awareness to your experience during the date itself, particularly anxious thoughts about how the evening is going. Notice these thoughts and allow them to fall away without getting caught up in their content. Also, whenever necessary, ground yourself in your breath and body sensations (the feeling of your feet on the floor, your hands on the table, sensations in your lower back, shoulders and neck).

Perhaps remind yourself that the other person almost certainly feels nervous too. To some extent, we all get nervous on dates.

After: Without blame or judgment, if possible, reflect on how the evening went. Congratulate yourself on the fact that you formed the intention to be mindful throughout. Notice any tendency to pick apart moments during the date that were not particularly satisfying. Remind yourself that no date is ever perfect and that there's always a next time.

I have almost finished the course now and I feel it's genuinely been life-changing. If it has worked for me I figure it might work for my friends, many of whom live very anxious lives. But I can't seem to get any of them interested in meditation.
Any ideas?

It can be difficult to convince someone of the benefits of meditation if they have a firm resistance to it.

Ultimately, all we can do is embody mindfulness in our daily actions. Either it rubs off on people or it doesn't.

As we all know from experience, mindfulness will find you when the time is right. If the time isn't right, no amount of enthusiasm will convince someone to look into it.

So, be the evidence. But remember it's not up to you what someone else thinks, and neither should it be. There is no shortage of people who are open to these ideas and techniques, perhaps it would be more worthwhile to find and help them?

?

Just a quick question about the guided meditations. I've finished week seven of the course now and fancy having a go at meditating without using the audios during my final week. Is that OK?

Absolutely.

Guided meditations are particularly useful for beginners but some meditators continue using them as they progress in their practice. There is nothing wrong with that. It comes down to personal preferences. For one thing, many people find it very difficult to do body scans without some guidance.

Feel free to carry on using the guided meditations as long as that feels comfortable for you.

Unguided meditations are a useful step to experiment with and can be deeply insightful and rewarding. You could maybe use less guided meditations (which usually have longer silent periods in them) as a halfway house.

As I approach the end of this course, a number of questions are bubbling up. Chief among them is this: what is happiness? I used to think I knew the answer.

Happiness was finding the right partner, having a well-paid job, being liked by my colleagues and friends, being able to take a couple of holidays each year…now I'm not so sure. I'm starting to sense that maybe happiness, true happiness, runs a lot deeper than having those things sorted in one's life. What do you think?

Most of us, at least in the west, have been conditioned to believe that happiness will be found in those things you name. But mindfulness can help us to look deeper, and further. Perhaps we begin to realise that it's easy to confuse pleasure with happiness.

Certain things bring us pleasure but how many of them can truly be said to bring us lasting happiness? Maybe true happiness is not dependent on anything outside of ourselves.

It is more about being comfortable within our own bodies; being properly reconciled with ourselves; living with a sense of quiet presence; feeling at home in the world; freeing ourselves from the illusion of who we think we are; living more authentically; being able to live our lives as though they really matter rather than acting as though life is a rehearsal.

With practice, mindfulness opens us up to all those possibilities. And more.

I have a problem with judging. As much as I try, I find it hard to let go of thoughts about what is good or bad, right or wrong. I've been brought up with strict ideas about these things. How do I let go of judgments?

With gentle and self-compassionate practice.

Judging is a habit, a deeply-conditioned one for most of us. Mindfulness invites us to see through those judgments or, at least, to carry them a little lighter. If we can learn to do that, there is less likelihood of being harsh towards ourselves and those around us.

As Alan Watts wrote: 'Things are as they are. Looking out into the universe at night, we make no comparisons between

right and wrong stars, nor between well and badly arranged constellations.'

Take that as your starting point. See if it is possible, even for just a moment or two, to see that things are as they are. Because, when we learn to let things be, just as they are, we learn to let go of them.

This course has definitely made me calmer and kinder to myself (and others most of the time). But I still seem to be stuck in certain habits. I get angry a lot, especially when my boyfriend is not listening to me. And I still spend far too much time on my smartphone and on Facebook. Isn't mindfulness supposed to 'undo' those bad habits?

A. Mindfulness can certainly help to undo habits but it can take time, patience and plenty of loving-kindness.
It's a fact of life that the more we repeat thoughts and actions, the more likely we are to keep repeating them, even if those thoughts and actions cause us suffering. These habits include craving, distractions, resistance and unnecessary worry.

Most habits are not obvious to us. They are unconscious, working deep under the radar as we go about our daily lives. We don't choose our habits and many of our longest-held habits don't serve our best interests.

How often do we find ourselves thinking, 'Why do I keep doing this?' as we carry on doing exactly that – whether it's smoking, drinking, eating unhealthily, choosing partners and friends, losing our cool, judging others…

Many of us seem to become trapped in the familiarity of our suffering. Deep inside, we are aware that the choices we continue to make bring us unhappiness but we continue to make those choices as though, somehow, we find a comfort in the familiarity of our discomfort.

We may not like the difficulties and dissatisfaction that certain choices bring but we continue to make those choices because we are strangely comfortable in our discomfort. Preferring the familiar to the unknown, we continue to make decisions that promote turmoil in our lives.

Already, you are aware that these habits are persisting. That's a great start. Take another look at the before/during/

after approach explained in the pdf for week one and form the intention of paying attention to the specific habit in those ways.

This course has definitely brought me many benefits but I'm not sure that I'm bringing enough attention to things in my everyday life. It's as though I get caught up in my thoughts about what I need to do next and I forget to be mindful. It happens a lot when I'm travelling to work on the bus.

I just can't seem to resist checking my phone every few minutes to see if my boss has emailed me with plans for the day or whether my girlfriend has left a nice message. How do I pay attention better?

There's a story about paying attention involving the great Austrian poet, Rainer Maria Rilke. Working as secretary to the great sculptor, Augusta Rodin, Rilke temporarily lost the ability to write. To Rodin, that meant that Rilke had stopped seeing, had stopped paying attention. He suggested that the poet go to Paris Zoo every day, choose one animal, study it in all its movements and moods until he knew it as thoroughly as a creature or thing could be known, then write

about it. The result was The Panther, one of Rilke's towering masterpieces and a great feat of poetic observation.

We may not be able to write poetry as sublime as Rilke but might we be able to pay attention to what is around us as closely as Rilke paid attention in the Paris zoo?

It doesn't mean that you need to visit a zoo. Next time you are on the bus, why not put your phone away and form the intention of being attentive to your experience for a few minutes? Notice your breathing. Register any sensations in your body.

Bring your curiosity to the other people in the bus and to the scenery outside. You're not looking for anything special to happen. You are simply being present in your moment-to-moment experience.

What am I meant to be aware of in the moment? I mean, it's not possible to be aware of everything, right?

Of course, it is impossible to pay attention to everything that is occurring in the moment.

You are not 'meant' to be aware of anything in particular. Whatever takes 'centre stage' in your focus is what you are chiefly aware of.

But there's a danger in over-thinking mindfulness to the point where someone can convince themselves they need to be mindful 24/7. That can lead to more self-consciousness and less mindfulness.

Think about it this way: every moment is an invitation to be mindful.

We don't go looking for mindfulness 'experiences'. We can form the intention to be mindful when attending to work, showering, brushing teeth etc. Or we can catch ourselves being unmindful and, in that gentle noticing, our practice comes to the fore.

We notice whatever our senses pick up in the moment. It might be a smell, a sense of touch, something that catches the eye etc.

In the 'choiceless awareness' meditation, we are invited to do just that: allowing our attention to go wherever it is drawn.

With mindfulness I'm learning to appreciate my life a lot more. But I'm still finding it a little difficult to completely switch off when, for example, I'm in the world of nature. I can be walking through a beautiful woods with my dog on a Sunday morning and find that my thoughts have a habit of getting in the way.

It's as though I'm spending more time thinking about nature than actually experiencing it. Is there anything I can do to feel more connected to the wider world?

Just keep practicing. If you are already beginning to appreciate your life more, the chances are that this appreciation will, in time, extend to your appreciation of nature.

Perhaps try a breathing space when you are out and about and see what difference that makes. It's still early days and, remember, mindfulness is for life. Chances are that the veil

of thinking will gradually lift and you will find it easier an easier to be in rapport with everything around you.

A sense of wonder is our birthright. As we become adults, many of us have a tendency to lose touch with that sense. It only needs to be cultivated. As we become more aware, we are able to more easily open up to the enchantment of the world around us.

SESSION EIGHT: EVERYDAY MINDFULNESS

'When we dance, the journey itself is the point, as when we play music the playing itself is the point. Exactly the same thing is true in meditation. Meditation is the discovery that the point of life is always arrived at in the immediate moment.' (Alan Watts)

'Have patience with everything that remains unsolved in your heart. Try to love the questions themselves, like locked rooms and like books written in a foreign language. Do not now look for the answers. They cannot now be given to you because you could not live them. It is a question of experiencing everything. At present you need to live the question. Perhaps you will gradually, without even noticing it, find yourself experiencing the answer, some distant day.'
(Rainer Maria Rilke)

Theme For Session Eight

In the final week of the eight-week course we look back on what we have learnt in previous weeks and look ahead to how best we can maintain practice.

Remember. This course lasts eight weeks. The ninth week is the rest of your life.

We are here to support you in that.

As we enter the eighth week of the course, let us have a quick recap of some of the main areas we've been exploring in the past seven weeks:

* Bringing awareness to your present moment experience, whether it is pleasant, unpleasant or somewhere in between. Learning to hold that experience in the transitional space of bare attention.

* Maintaining an attitude or intention of openness and curiosity.

* Meeting each and every experience with compassion and acceptance.

* Reminding ourselves that all experiences, even unpleasant ones, pass. Reminding ourselves that life is change. Life is constant motion.

* Gently letting go of expectations, thoughts and judgments.

* Realising that you are not your thoughts. Appreciating that thoughts are not facts. In seeing these truths, thoughts tend to lose their charge. They come to be seen as passing neurological events, mere secretions of the mind, subconscious gossip.

It is not thoughts that imprison us but the authority we give them. When thoughts are held in awareness, they tend to lose their hold over us and so we are able to emerge from the trance of thinking.

* Realising that being mindful in your life doesn't require much. A commitment to practice. A motivated engagement. A chair to meditate on. Patience. That's about it. We begin, again and again if necessary, with the simple intention of being mindful.

By now you will almost certainly have noticed how the Turning Point mindfulness course has helped you build the foundations of a sustained personal practice and now you are starting to notice the benefits of mindfulness.

The importance of committing to a continued practice cannot be underestimated. Make it a priority to carve out a regular practice time. But be gentle and compassionate with yourself at all times.

From time to time, you might find it tough going. Especially when life is confronting you with tough challenges. Spiritual teacher Ram Dass asks, 'Can you keep your heart open in hell?'

In other words, can we turn kindly towards our experience when life is dealing out those tough challenges?

There may be days when staying with the discomfort that arises in these situations proves a little too much. If so, remember not to push yourself too hard. Turn towards difficulty only when you feel up to it.

If today is not the day for turning towards unpleasant thoughts and feelings in meditation, simply focus on your breath, and try again tomorrow.

If you find yourself occasionally lapsing in your practice, you won't have been the first to do so. It happens to practically all of us at some time or other.

Most of us are creatures of habit. We can just as easily fall into the habit of not doing something as doing something. If we go a couple of days without meditating for whatever reason, this can easily turn into a week, a fortnight, a month…After a while, not meditating becomes the habit.

You might notice yourself avoiding the opportunity to practice, finding countless reasons why not to, and compiling endless mental lists of other more important things which demand your time. This is a prime moment to remember self-compassion – not to give yourself a hard time, but to gently return to your practice. Just as you would gently return to the breath when you get distracted in a meditation.

Accept that, from time to time, your practice will lose its focus, sometimes a little, sometimes a lot.

At times like these, remind yourself of why you were drawn to mindfulness in the first place and what your intentions were at that time. This can provide a sense of direction and purpose which can radically re-energise your practice.

Sometimes people find that their practice lapses because they are reaping the benefits of mindfulness practice and not because they've run into problems with it.

If a regular meditation practice is making you less anxious or less depressed, more accepting and self-aware, more appreciative of life in general, it may be tempting to think that mindfulness has done the trick and that you can afford to allow the formal meditation to slide.

When that happens, hold to the intention to begin again. If necessary, re-do our eight-week course. Or, better still, sign up to our ongoing Ninth Week course. About which, more later.

Jon Kabat-Zinn has compared mindfulness practice to weaving a parachute. We don't want to start practicing when we are in difficulty and need to jump out of the plane. We want to be weaving the parachute day and night, just hoping that, when we need the support of mindfulness practice, it has a better chance of supporting us.

This is why it's wonderful to enjoy meditation rather than think of it as a chore – that way, we have the win-win situation.

Remember. Mindfulness is not a skill that we master and then have no further need to practice. It is a way of being and therefore an ongoing practice.

Every moment is an opportunity to not only be mindful but to cultivate the practice more deeply. Think of mindfulness as a 'muscle' that benefits from regular exercise and yourself as the blessedly lucky recipient of those benefits.

In a very real sense, every moment is a potential turning point.

Throughout the eight-week course you have been reminded to adopt an attitude of patience, curiosity and open mindedness. Continuing with that attitude as your practice extends into the rest of your life would be no bad thing.

But we realise that it's often easier said than done.
Here are a few tips for maintaining practice or returning to practice when you have lapsed for a while.

* Keep your practice fresh.

It's easy to fall into a routine of only doing the meditations you like the most or find easiest. That might be sitting meditation or the body scan, mindful movement or walking meditation. Try shaking up your practice once in a while.

As with just about anything in life, a bit of variation is always a positive thing.

Throw in a few body scans if you haven't done one for a while. Do more sitting meditation if you have been concentrating mostly on body scans. Practice some form of mindful movement a few times each week. Walk mindfully whenever you can.

* Join a meet-up group

If none of your close circle of friends is interested in meditation, it can be quite isolating. Why not check out whether there are any mindfulness meet-up groups in your area? Failing that, why not start your own with meet-up.com? Groups are easy to set up and cheap to run. It's a

great way of meeting like-minded people and you can organise group meditations with them if you like.

* Use Everyday Mindfulness.

Our companion website, Everyday Mindfulness, is the biggest mindfulness site in the world. As well as great resources (interviews, blogs, tons of useful information and links, Facebook page etc.) it also has a very lively interactive forum where you can ask questions and share ideas about mindfulness. https://www.everyday-mindfulness.org

* Use mindfulness triggers.

Employ natural mindfulness triggers during the day to bring your attention back to the present moment: when the phone rings, when you stop at traffic lights, when the kettle boils. Use these moments to take a breath and to come into body sensation.

Notice when you are rushing or hurrying. Bring awareness to your state of mind, emotions and body sensations in these moments. When you find yourself waiting or queuing for

something, use these moments as valuable opportunities to stop and tune into your experience.

Continue to choose daily activities that you can conduct consciously with mindful attention: brushing your teeth, doing the washing up, getting dressed. Pay full attention to what you are doing and, when the mind wanders, bring it back. Enjoy the different perspective, the richer detail and the greater intimacy this brings.

* Before falling asleep at night, bring awareness to your breathing and your body sensations for at least five whole breaths, all the way in and all the way out.

* Watch what you eat.

If you can, be more careful about what you put in your mouth every day. No junk food. Fewer animal products and fewer processed foods. Less refined carbohydrates. More plants, vegetables and legumes. More fresh fruit. More water. Less alcohol, less sugary drinks and 'energy' drinks. Rediscover the joy of eating by being more present at each stage of a meal, from deciding what it is that you want to eat to washing up and tidying away.

When you eat or drink, bring awareness to the process of smelling, tasting, sensing and nourishing yourself. In this way, you can turn mealtimes into acts of love and benefit accordingly.

* Open a book.

One way of maintaining your mindfulness practice is to read some relevant books. Here are some titles we would warmly recommend to those who have finished the eight-week course:

Jon Kabat-Zinn: Full Catastrophe Living
Jon Kabat-Zinn: Coming To Our Senses
Stephan Bodian: Beyond Mindfulness – The Direct Approach To Lasting Peace, Happiness & Love
Eckhart Tolle: The Power Of Now
Eckhart Tolle: A New Earth
Ed Halliwell: Into The Heart Of Mindfulness
Adyashanti: True Meditation
Danny Penman: The Art Of Breathing
Danny Penman: Mindfulness For Creativity

Elisha Goldstein: Uncovering Happiness – Overcoming Depression With Mindful And Self-Compassion

Sharon Salzberg: Lovingkindness – The Revolutionary Art Of Kindness

Christina Feldman: Boundless Heart

Christina Feldman: Compassion – Listening To The Cries Of The World

Saki Santorelli: Heal Thy Self - Lessons On Mindfulness In Medicine

Vidyamala Burch & Danny Penman: Mindfulness For Health – A Practical Guide To Relieving Pain, Reducing Stress & Restoring Wellbeing

Richard Gilpin: Mindfulness For Black Dogs & Blue Days – Finding A Path Through Depression

Richard Gilpin: Mindfulness For Unravelling Anxiety – Finding Calm & Clarity In Uncertain Times

Claire Thompson: Mindfulness & The Natural World

The ninth week is the rest of your life.

For many people, an eight-week mindfulness course is over and done with all too soon. Just as they are beginning to get a firm grounding in mindfulness, the course is completed, leaving them feeling a little rudderless.

That's why we have developed the Ninth Week course specifically for those who have already benefitted from mindfulness and who wish to continue to be supported in their practice.

As with the eight week course, we have aimed to make the Ninth Week course accessible to as many people as possible and to deliver it in a purely secular way whilst maintaining the integrity of ancient meditation teachings upon which modern-day mindfulness is based.

You'll find details of the Ninth Week course on our website.

It's been a pleasure being with you these past eight weeks. Thank you for being with us. We hope you will stick around and allow us to help you nurture the seed of mindfulness.

Long may mindfulness flourish and grow in your life.

'When it's over, I want to say: all my life
I was a bride married to amazement
I was the bridegroom, taking the world into my arms.'
(Mary Oliver)

Home practice for week following session eight

Body Scan Meditation

Listen to the longer (40 minute) Body Scan guided meditation on three of the next seven days.

Choose Your Own!

On three of the next seven days, choose your own daily meditations from those you have been introduced to on this course.

A Day Of Mindfulness

Throughout this eight-week course, we have suggested you do home practice on six of the seven days.

This week, the final week, is a little different.

On the seventh day, the one you would normally 'take off', you are invited to dedicate yourself to a whole nourishing day of mindfulness.

This could be an ordinary quiet day at home, or an 'awayday' somewhere special. The important thing is that you do not try to do too much and, what you do engage in, you do with mindfulness.

It may work best for you if you aim to experience the time alone, or as alone as possible.

You can decide to turn the radio and television off, and restrict how much you absorb yourself in books, newspapers and music. You can put the telephone on silent/answering mode so you will not be disturbed.

We are setting up time for being with ourselves in a way that we do not usually have time for, free from our usual demands, obligations and pressures. It is free time which we are not going to rush to fill.

We may want to engage in some simple and focused activities which will not make us lose touch with ourselves: perhaps some walking or mindful movement. We may wish to read poetry or spend time with nature.

This day of guided practice is an opportunity to immerse ourselves more deeply into the mindfulness practices we have been building up over the past few weeks.

NUTRITION - Week Eight: Ten Strategies To Support A Healthy Mind

What we eat is important, and so is the way we eat. Mindfulness is the key to healthy eating - being conscious of each bite, savouring the taste and appreciating the nourishment it provides for our bodies and minds.

For this final session, I have created a top ten list of the most effective nutritional and lifestyle strategies to support a healthy mind:

1 - Rehydrate regularly throughout the day: 6 to 8 glasses of water or herbal tea (add a slice of lemon or lime if preferred). In addition to proper hydration, ensure adequate sleep, daily exercise and increase fresh air and sunlight.

"In one drop of water are found all the secrets of the oceans."- Khalil Gibran

2 - Support your digestion by eating slowly and chewing your food well. Speedy, careless eating encourages digestive problems and affects how you feel. If you are in a stressful situation or environment, either eat later or remove

yourself to a peaceful, quiet place and take a few deep belly breaths before eating.

"Every day brings a choice: to practice stress or to practice peace." – Joan Borysenko.

3 - The bacterial flora in your gut affects your mental health. Your 'friendly' bugs thrive on a healthy diet. This means a diet high in plant fibre containing a high nutrient density, vitamins, minerals, antioxidants and phytonutrients. Look for a variety of fresh, colourful, local and seasonal produce. Try to eat 5-8 portions of vegetables per day (raw, steamed or stir-fried) and 2 portions of fruit.

"We should all be eating fruits and vegetables as if our lives depend on it – because they do." – Michael Greger, MD

4 - Buy whole basic ingredients of high quality to clean, assemble, cook and bake at home. Avoid refined grains and eat a variety of wholegrain products. Whole grains consist of the entire grain seed of a plant, including the bran, germ and endosperm.

"Make food simple and let things taste of what they are."- Maurice Edmond Sailland

5 - Read labels and look for items that do not have a long list of chemical additives with unpronounceable names (check drinks, toothpaste and medicines as well). Avoid added salt (sodium chloride) or salty convenience foods.

"Give neither counsel nor salt till you are asked for it." – English Proverb

6 - Wheat, barley, rye and triticale contain a protein called gluten. Some people are gluten-intolerant, and it can affect not only their digestion and immune systems, but also their brains. Oats do not contain gluten, but may be contaminated with gluten (you can buy gluten-free oats). Quinoa, amaranth, buckwheat, corn, millet, brown or wild rice, sorghum and teff are all gluten-free.

"Gluten is this generation's tobacco." — David Perlmutter

7 - Eat quality protein every day (meat, fish, eggs, dairy from reputable sources). If vegetarian or vegan, choose wholegrains, beans and pulses.

"Most people naturally eat the right amount of protein for their needs. Protein is such a crucial nutrient that the brain has specific mechanisms that increase your desire for it if you need more and decrease your desire for it if you're getting too much; these mechanisms are difficult to override through willpower alone. " – Chris Kresser

8 - Eat the right fats. Avoid hydrogenated and deep-fried fats. The oils in nuts, seeds, avocados and olives are highly beneficial. The omega-3 oils in fish even more so: eat two to four portions of fish per week. Choose small, unpolluted oily fish including sprats, sild, whitebait, anchovies and sardines.

"No diet will remove all the fat from your body because the brain is entirely fat. Without a brain, you might look good, but all you could do is run for public office." - George Bernard Shaw, 1856-1950

9 - Eat regular meals and try to have breakfast, even if it's just fruit and nuts. Avoid common blood sugar disrupters: sugar and other forms of concentrated sweetness (including artificial sweeteners), caffeine, nicotine, alcohol, stress.

"The facts are in, the science is beyond question. Sugar in all its forms is the root cause of our obesity epidemic and most of the chronic disease sucking the life out of our citizens and our economy — and, increasingly, the rest of the world. You name it, it's caused by sugar: heart disease, cancer, dementia, type 2 diabetes, depression, and even acne, infertility and impotence." – Dr Mark Hyman

10 - Identify any suspected food intolerances, nutritional imbalances or exposure to pollutants with the help of a Registered Nutritional Therapist. We have access to reliable testing procedures and can support you on your journey to improved mood, focus and concentration.

"The primary seat of insanity generally is in the region of the stomach and intestines." - Philippe Pinel (French psychiatrist, 1745-1826)

All of us deserve to find strategies to live a life of quality and presence that works. Although innovation and progress are necessary, some of the valuables we sacrifice for the sake of convenient lives and convenience foods may turn out to be the most essential.

This sentiment was beautifully expressed by Caroline Walker, a tireless campaigner for "real" food who died when she was 38 years old: "Good food is part of the joy of life. Good food, farmed and grown well, creates beautiful landscapes, respects wildlife and encourages pride in work. Good cooking is integral to family life. The culinary arts are part of civilisation."

Disclaimer:

Please do NOT stop taking any medication without prior consultation with your doctor. Also, be aware that de-junking your diet can make you feel worse before you feel better, due to withdrawal symptoms or poor liver detoxification. Make any changes to your diet slowly and seek professional advice from a Registered Nutritional Therapist.

Contact martina@thehealthbank.co.uk for more information or visit www.thehealthbank.co.uk

Jon's reflections on his first eight-week course.

It is said that people come to mindfulness either by way of a whisper or a scream. By the time I was ready to give it a go, I was more at the 'scream' end of the spectrum. I was desperately unhappy in my life, regularly suffering from deep depression and near constant anxiety. I pretty much felt at the end of my rope, aware that the life I was living was unsustainable.

Having decided to give mindfulness a shot, I approached the first session of my course with a great deal of hope (that it would 'work') and an equal amount of cynicism (that it wouldn't).

By and large, I hit the ground running with it, largely I suspect because I was absolutely ready for it.

In the first fortnight, I started to notice that my mind was wandering less and less during meditation, a sign that I was already beginning to strengthen the muscles of awareness and attention. My mind continued to wander during meditation but I noticed that I was becoming less judgmental in that respect.

As the course continued, I was finding it easier to take to my bench to meditate and to fold meditation into my daily routine. Meditation was becoming more effortless. Less and less did I find myself thinking, 'When will this be over? I need to get on with my day.' Or, when I did find myself having those thoughts, they were becoming easier to let go of.

Meanwhile, I was finding it easier to drop into present moment awareness during the day and adopt a much broader perspective on situations I found myself in.

Slowly but surely, I noticed that I was starting to break some of my unconscious habits of behaving and thinking. I no longer felt depressed. My anxiety was less intense.

Then reality reared up and took a bite out of me. After a couple of freelance jobs fell through, I faced some serious cash flow problems. Short-term problems, but ones that sent my anxiety into orbit. Depression began to nibble around the edges.

Meditation didn't seem to help, but I stuck with it. I was overwhelmed with worry. 'What if I don't have enough

money to last me the month? What if work dries up completely? How will I survive?'
I kept meditating. I started to see some daylight. I could borrow a little money from friends to see me through the month. Maybe work will pick up? It did. I kept meditating. The storm passed.

The experience was a sharp reminder that I shouldn't expect too much of mindfulness too soon. I needed to allow it to unfold in its own time. Like a concert pianist playing key phrases of music over and over, or a surgeon learning how to apply exactly the right amount of pressure to a suture, it would take time to hone my attentive skills.

It doesn't magically happen overnight, between one meditation and another. The effect is cumulative.

I was reminded of another of my old nan's sayings:
'If you take care of the minutes, the years will take care of themselves.'

I made the intention to be patient. And kinder to myself.

Around the halfway point of the course, I noticed that I was becoming a little less attached to outcomes. Slowly I was

beginning to accept the idea that, while life won't always turn out the way I hope it will, it might be possible to notice that the present moment is abundant enough as it is if I drop all ideas about how it should be. When I felt the need for the moment to be something other than what it was, I got into the habit of taking a mindful pause and asking myself, 'What is this moment lacking?' Or I would take a short breathing space, resting in awareness for a few minutes.

More and more, I could see that I didn't have to constantly react to whatever life presents. That it is OK to simply be and to welcome life as it arrives, moment after moment, being as open to it as I can.

Occasionally I would remind myself of the world famous Serenity Prayer: 'The grace to accept with serenity the things that cannot be changed. The courage to change the things that should be changed. The wisdom to distinguish one from the other.' Accepting that there were always going to be things that I couldn't change was sometimes challenging, but the truth of it slowly bedded in.

All this was supporting a more mindful way of being. A way of being with what is, as it is. Allowing things to be just as they are. Just this. When we learn to let things be,

just as they are, we learn to let go of them. It was becoming apparent to me that true freedom is more a case of liking what we get than getting what we like.

I was always quite taken by the title of George Harrison's 1970 solo album, All Things Must Pass, unaware that it was adapted from the ancient Persian adage, 'this too shall pass.' However, I never quite grasped the full import of the expression. Grounding myself in mindfulness, I could see that so much of my suffering arose because I couldn't or wouldn't accept the inevitably transient nature of existence. I needed to see that nothing was fixed, even for a moment, that everything is change. Everything comes and goes.

The Buddha said, 'Everything that comes to be must pass away; make your peace with this and all will be well.' This would take some time to sink in. A greater sense of peace didn't come overnight. Gradually though, it sank in that, when my moment to moment experience was held in gentle awareness, difficult thoughts and feelings of sadness, loneliness and confusion were simply experiences arising and not the totality of what I am or who I am.

When this was fully realised, I was no longer engaged in a constant fight with the universe. I could be with the flow

that life is, and move within it. Instead of holding my breath, wanting certain things to be permanent, fixed, I could breathe and let be.

As my practice continued, I felt more grounded in my body and, without a shadow of a doubt, I was spending less time living in my head. Less time doing, more time being. Less striving, more non-doing. Less reactive, more responsive. Less time spent trying to fix the past and worrying about what the future will bring.

I was becoming more and more mindful of what I was eating and how I consumed my food. An inveterate snacker I learned to check myself when I reached for that mid-morning chocolate éclair or that mid-afternoon packet of cheese & onion crisps.

I cut out junk food altogether and drastically cut down on processed foods. I refined my diet to include less refined carbohydrates, more plants, vegetables and legumes, more fresh fruit, more whole grains. I drank more water. Less alcohol, less sugary drinks and 'energy' drinks. My friends told me I looked ten years younger and I almost believed them.

It wasn't all plain sailing. Around the seventh week of the course, I encountered a few difficulties. Work dried up (again). I had a falling out with a close friend who I felt had betrayed my trust. Running for a bus, I fell and sprained my ankle.

For a couple of days, I didn't meditate at all. Anxious thoughts trickled and then gushed, colouring everything a deep shade of grey.

I started meditating again and vowed to cultivate a different relationship to my current worries. I told myself that work would doubtlessly pick up, and it did (again).

As sore as I felt about the behaviour of my friend, I reminded myself that he was having a difficult time after his girlfriend left him. I called him and invited him out for a coffee. We made up.

My ankle was sore and it hurt when I walked. It made meditation more challenging. I reminded myself that it was only a sprain and the pain…that too would pass. And, of course, it did.

Even when days were challenging, I was able to comfort myself with the knowledge that I had planted a seed, a seed of intention to live mindfully and be awake. Moment by moment by moment. Day by day by day.

What's more, I could clearly see the benefits that mindfulness had already brought. A deeper sense of wellbeing, a greater sense of wholeness, a feeling of waking up to the fullness of my life. I remember lying in bed one night thinking that I had begun to come home to myself in a very meaningful way.

Perhaps the most profound change in me was a feeling of being more awake to the wonder of the world, being reacquainted with the magic of everyday life as if I'd been reborn as a young, carefree child with a long summer holiday stretching before me.

Like the child, can we fully inhabit the experience we are in? Can we allow ourselves to feel awe at the simple fact of being alive in this moment? Can we be astonished at the sheer majesty of an oak tree? Can we be enchanted by the sight of a flowing river? Can we be uplifted when our eyes alight on morning dew? Can we be transfixed by the movement of a tiny insect?

Like Albert Einstein, can we admire in humility the beautiful harmony of the structure of this world as far as we can grasp it? Can we see the world as if for the first time rather than act as though we have seen it all before which happens when our attention grows thin? Can we rediscover the magic of wonderment and be profoundly grateful for it?

Mindfulness teaches us that the wonders of the universe are right in front of us every day. We don't need esoteric beliefs to appreciate what the universe has to offer. As naturalist Chet Raymo writes in his acclaimed book, The Path: 'Why should we care about angels when the season's first blackbirds spread their red-shouldered wings? Why should we seek treasures in Heaven when year after year the fiddlehead ferns unfurl their silver croziers along the brook? Why should we look for out-of-body experiences when it is our bodies that connect us to the sights, sounds, tastes, smells and tactile sensations of nature? The smallest insect is more worthy of our astonishment than a thousand sprites or poltergeists.'

Towards the end of my first mindfulness course, I knew deep in my bones that the practice was helping me to reconnect to a sense of aliveness I hadn't truly felt since I

was a kid. I was reclaiming my sense of wonder. And it felt…wonderful.

Paying attention to our experience as it is unfolding, all of it has the potential to be endlessly interesting. To endless delight, I discovered that even moments of boredom, when observed mindfully, can be utterly fascinating. Bringing our bare attention to the feelings of boredom and associated thoughts, we might see that, when we are bored, we are skimming along the surface of experience. We are unengaged. We find ourselves between one thing and another, suspended in mid-air, needing to do rather than be.

If we pay sufficient attention, we might notice that it is not the moment that is boring, it is what we bring to it. If we can ground ourselves in the moment, letting go of thoughts about how this moment is lacking somehow, we may allow ourselves to become interested in the sights, smells and sounds around us, recognizing the world just as it is, realizing that every moment is precious.

Another thing. Mindfulness was helping me become more attuned to the interconnectedness of all things. I started to see that the sense of myself as an entity separate from the rest of the universe was, as Einstein put it, a kind of optical

delusion of my consciousness. When that was seen, it suddenly became more possible to walk with compassion, with everybody and everything on a common path.

Again, I didn't discover a whole new way of being overnight. It came with sustained practice. The more I practiced, the more it was possible to experience life through a wide lens rather than a narrow one. Mindfulness also cleared the lens so that I was able to pay bare attention to my moment to moment experience, rather than experiencing life through the unreliable filter of mental concepts.

Mindfulness started as something that I did. Now it's who I am.

It's an ongoing process, aided and abetted by daily practice. It's a continuous adventure, one that becomes more and more effortless.

But remember, everyone's mindfulness journey is unique. Your adventure will be your own adventure. Don't despair if you find that you are not experiencing the same changes I have described above. Fold mindfulness into your life in

your own way. Be your own light. Be awake in your own incomparable way. And keep practicing.

GERARD'S REFLECTIONS ON WEEK EIGHT

As I sit at the computer to write this final reflection on the course, many things have changed.

Take how I sit at the computer, for instance. I used to flop down on the chair and sit with terrible posture, ending up with a permanently stiff neck and a course of physiotherapy at the local hospital.

Now I make a little ritual of making sure my chair is at the right height, making sure I'm comfortable. I turn off my email and my phone and give my attention fully to the task in hand. I clean my specs and gently but firmly set my intention for the coming hour. All little aspects of skilful living that add up to far more than the sum of their parts.

In writing about how mindfulness has encouraged me towards practical changes in my life, I hope to illustrate how you could do similarly. Your ways will, of course, be completely different, as unique to you as mine are to me.

But hopefully the general principles can shine through the examples.

* * *

I think it's important to point out that I haven't turned into some perfect goody-goody who floats through life in an enlightened glow. I still get things wrong - but accept my failings with far more loving- kindness and far less harsh criticism. Wrong doesn't hurt anymore.

I've presented the best side of myself in these reflections because I believe that's the most useful thing to do, but I don't want to pretend I've become faultless or that my life has become a stress-free bliss-zone.

That's not what this course is about - it's not a competition to see who can be the most enlightened, or even who can be the most mindful.

It's just a gentle way of learning and applying beautiful skills, one of which is the ability to gently forgive yourself when your attention wanders from them.

This will happen as surely as your attention wanders during a meditation. And the response is the same - treat yourself with love and compassion, don't waste energy on needless self-judgment all the time, just gently bring yourself back to the chosen direction and carry on.

With mindfulness, every time you bring your attention back, you are developing that muscle. Equally, anytime you 'fall off the wagon' with any given intention, you can bring yourself back without frustration or judgment and continue to develop the same muscle. It's a neat system that does away with the unhelpful concept of failure and replaces it with positive forward motion, even in times of distraction. Most of all, it works.

As Jon points out in his Week One reflection: 'I was greatly encouraged when my teacher remarked that the fact my mind was wandering didn't mean I was doing it wrong.' This is a revolutionary shift in our taught attitude and one that I feel will live with me forever. Like a benign parent.

If you get even half what I've got out of this course, then your life will change forever, for the better. You'll never look back, at least not back in anger or regret. That's kind of the point really, isn't it?

So please, take the skills and techniques presented in this book - as ancient as the human condition but adapted for modern life - and use them as you will, molding them to fit your own set of circumstances. If they help you half as much as they've helped me, then you will possess the ability to transform your life in pretty much any direction you fancy. It's that powerful.

FAQ FOR WEEK EIGHT

Mindfulness is definitely making a difference in terms of my thinking.

At first I really struggled to try and clear my mind, and was actually very successful and could spend minutes at a time with a thoughtless mind.

It doesn't happen often though. A lot of the time my mind is still like a pinball machine!

Remember that we're not trying to stop thoughts from arising.

However much you practice, thoughts will continue to come and go just as clouds form and dissolve in the sky. There's no getting away from that. The blood circulates. The hair grows. The breath ebbs and flows. Thoughts arrive in consciousness, then depart.
Ultimately, it's about noticing thoughts without becoming attached to their content. The mind loves to weave a narrative.

Mindfulness teaches us that we have a choice; that we can be aware of the thought stream without being dragged away by it.

We can accept that thoughts have already arrived and, without any frustration or judgment, return our attention to the breath, or whatever anchor we choose.

If we think of mindfulness as a way of honing the muscle of awareness, then the pinball machine effect you mention can be thought of as the optimum workout.
Practice is, of course, key.

I was thinking this morning: I wish I'd started mindfulness sooner. I'm 44 now. I could have done with these skills when I was sixteen! I wonder if anyone else feels the same?

I imagine most of us have thought something similar at one time or another. I guess mindfulness finds us when we are ready for it. It's not a thought worth dwelling on though. As we have learnt during the course, Now is all. This present moment is the only moment we have. We cannot live our lives backwards.

My point is that mindfulness seems much more to do with undoing old habits (esp. thinking habits) than creating new ones. Does that sound vaguely correct?

In truth, it's a bit of both.

Our minds are conditioned to behave the way they do. We've spent our entire lives being at the mercy of our thought patterns.

Mindfulness teaches us that we don't need to live that way. But, in the process, we need to be extremely gentle and patient with ourselves. Slowly but surely, with regular practice, healthier habits become the norm. This way, old habits undo themselves without our conscious effort being so much to the fore.

The more I practice mindfulness the more I get a sense that time is slowing down.

I wondered if anyone else had noticed that? Or is it just me?

If our lives are spent out of the moment (ruminating on the past, speculating about the future; or constantly thinking about the next thing that needs to be done), that can create a feeling that life is whizzing by. We might find ourselves heading to bed and thinking, 'Where did that day go?' As though it's been stolen from us.

Mindfulness teaches us that the only moment is now. If we spend a frantic day rushing from one task to the next, we'll feel that the day has rushed by in a blur, that we haven't actually lived it.

On days like that it might be worth us asking, 'Have I have a single moment of stillness today? Have I enjoyed a single moment where I've appreciated the fact that I am alive and that this moment will never come along again?'

What we may be able to do is stop ourselves living life at full-pelt without any meditative pause, so that we can cherish the moment from time to time. If we can live a little more in the moment, it's not that we're slowing time down, but we're not creating the illusion that time is speeding up.

A minute in stillness is just that – one minute. A minute of frantic thinking may only contain two seconds of stillness, making that minute effectively two seconds long. Thought of in that way, mindfulness can be a tool for stealing back your time as well as your life.

I have a question about goals.

I understand that we don't really have goals in mindfulness because we are not trying to get anywhere.

But what about goals in my life? I'd like to meet a nice lady, settle down and have some kids. I'd like to get a better paid job than the one I have now.

Is there something wrong with those kind of goals?

You are spot on about mindfulness and goals. As we begin to practice mindfulness, those goals tend to assume less urgency as we realise that mindfulness is not about striving for change. It's more about cultivating an awareness of what is already here.

In our lives, we just need to be careful about getting too attached to goals.

If you decide that you want a serious relationship, there's no harm in making decisions that will increase your chances of meeting the right person. eg. Joining a dating agency.

But there's a potential danger in buying into the idea that the perfect partner will turn up immediately and that you'll live happily ever after. It might take a number of dates before you meet someone suitable. And, even then, she is unlikely to be the perfect human being. Sadly, perfect human beings don't exist – no matter how perfect someone might SEEM after a first date when everything went swimmingly.

So it pays to go about dating as mindfully as we can, accepting perhaps that it is not an exact science.

Goals are fine, necessary even, so long as we don't get attached to them in ways that become stressful and counter-productive.

Take a look at someone like Richard Branson and you'll see that it's possible to achieve a lot of goals in life without the presumption that they need to be accompanied by endless testosterone and/or stress.

Mindfulness can aid achievement through better, calmer decision-making. It is certainly not an obstacle to getting what you want in life – though it is always possible that what you want may change slightly as you become less dissatisfied with what you already have.

After finishing the eight-week course I started reading a few books, including Eckhart Tolle's A New Earth. Tolle seems to be talking about mindfulness a lot though, if memory serves, he doesn't actually use the word. Would you say that Tolle is a mindfulness writer or is he a spiritual writer?

Well spotted! Tolle does not use the word 'mindfulness' in his books although, clearly, at times, he is referring explicitly to mindfulness practice. His remit is somewhat broader than mindfulness and, certainly, he could reasonably be described as a 'spiritual' writer.

Although mindfulness can be taken up as part of a spiritual practice, it doesn't have to be.

As you might have noticed, this course has been taught from a purely secular point of view.

Having reached the end of the course, I'm amazed at how mindfulness has enriched so many areas of my life. And I'm still a beginner! But I keep asking myself, 'Can mindfulness help me cope with anything that comes up in my life?' Does it have limits in terms of its effectiveness?

We've yet to find any area of life that mindfulness cannot be applied to. During your childhood you might have played Rock, Paper, Scissors. Think of mindfulness as a form of Rock, Paper, Scissors in which you always win. Mindfulness is able to rise and meet any obstacle. No exceptions.

I'm now at the end of the eight-week course. It has brought me many benefits but I'm continuing to drink far more than is healthy for me. I'd like to continue with your Ninth Week course but I'm also tempted to try AA. Can mindfulness be practiced alongside something like AA without too many problems?

A. Absolutely. For some people, mindfulness can be effective but may be only one of several suitable complementary approaches, and it may enhance the effectiveness of therapy, medication, yoga, twelve-step approaches etc. Just be mindful about finding room in your life for more than one approach. Try not to take too much on.

THE TURNING POINT COURSE - RECAP

For those who have completed our 8-week course, here's a handy recap of the main points covered.

What is mindfulness?

Commonly, mindfulness is defined as, 'the awareness that emerges through paying attention on purpose, in the present moment, and non-judgmentally to the unfolding of experience moment by moment.'

As much as anything, mindfulness involves taking time and care to notice what already exists.

More simply put, mindfulness is about being aware. It's about paying attention and taking better care of ourselves in the moment. Resting in awareness, we become fully aware of what we are actually experiencing and, thus, life comes into clearer focus.

Mindfulness enhances life, mindlessness reduces it.

Mindfulness is not about trying to get anywhere else or about attaining some special state. It is about returning our attention to the present moment, accepting the moment as it is and not being attached to a specific outcome. It is about being more at home in the world and showing up in our own lives. It's about undoing the mental and emotional patterns that make us miserable.

Mindfulness shows us that we can only start from where we are, not from where we would most like to be.

So much of our suffering is caused not by what is actually happening to us but by the belief that what we are thinking is the truth.

You do not have to believe your thoughts. Mindfulness teaches us to notice thoughts simply as thoughts, as passing mental events. With practice, we can choose not to get caught up in their content.

Mindfulness will not eliminate life's pressures. It will not solve all our problems. It will not make all your pain miraculously disappear. But it can help us respond to those things in a calmer, more resourceful, more conscious

manner. Mindfulness doesn't fix the cards dealt, but it can greatly enhance our skill in how to play our hand.

Mindfulness enables us to tune in to our present moment experience and adopt a far more skilful and flexible relationship to what we find challenging or unpleasant.

We do this simply by dropping our attachment to the idea that this moment should be different from what it is and simply opening up to our present moment experience with curiosity, calmness and creativity.

By learning to experience the present moment as it really is, we develop the ability to step away from habitual, often unconscious emotional and physiological reactions to everyday events, see things as they really are, and respond to them wisely rather than on auto-pilot.

Even in the midst of great hurt, humiliation, shame, sadness and anger, we can observe our experience as it unfolds from moment to moment, thereby being much better placed to avoid feeling overwhelmed.

We can start to see that, with practice, all mental states and emotional states, even the most challenging ones, can be accepted and worked with.

When we learn to let things be, just as they are, we learn to let go of them.

When we begin to accept ourselves for who we are, we can begin to accept others for who they are. Loving-kindness promotes wellbeing for all. But it starts with you.

Mindfulness teaches us that the struggle to avoid discomfort is often what prolongs it.

Mindfulness is about turning towards our experience and not turning away. We learn to relate to our experience without aversion or grasping. With practice we learn to work with the attachments and aversions that arise by turning towards our experience as it unfolds with gentleness and curiosity.

Mindfulness invites us to see that life is neither good nor bad, right nor wrong. It just is, as it is.

In befriending difficulty, turning kindly towards it, rather than turning away from it, we develop more skillful ways of relating to troublesome experiences. In doing so, we need to remember to be gentle with ourselves.
Mindfulness helps to create a space between the perceived difficulty and our reaction to it.

As we bring greater attention to our experience in the moment, it's very possible that we begin to see our life situation in a clearer context and from a wider perspective.

It is important to remember that mindfulness is not a matter of how well we meditate in a chair or on a cushion. It is about how we live our lives. From day to day, moment to moment.

In a very real sense, mindfulness practice is what we do when we sit down to meditate or lie down to do a body scan. And the rest of the day is the meditation.
In other words, every moment of the day is an invitation to drop into present-moment awareness and adopt a much broader perspective on any situation you find yourself in.

Your mindfulness practice is whatever you are doing, experiencing the present moment directly, without that experience being filtered through fears, prejudices and judgments. It's about recognizing the world as it is, seeing your life as it is in all its everyday messiness, and finding freedom in that.

Printed in Great
Britain
by Amazon